Pastor Chefs

21 Day
No Complaining
Marriage Challenge

Pastors Bill and Cynthia Malone

SIGNALMAN PUBLISHING

Pastor Chefs 21 Day No Complaining Marriage Challenge
by Bill and Cynthia Malone

Signalman Publishing
www.signalmanpublishing.com
email: info@signalmanpublishing.com
Kissimmee, Florida
1-888-907-4423

ISBN: 978-1-940145-65-5 (paperback)
978-1-940145-66-2 (ebook)

Library of Congress Control Number: 2016950424

Printed in the United States of America

SIGNALMAN
PUBLISHING

We dedicate this book to our beautiful, intelligent and well-rounded children. Ryan Malone and Seneca Diggs will always hold our hearts and provide us reason to fight harder to set a positive example. We pray that our work in ministry and our pursuit of the various dreams as husband and wife provide inspiration and example for our children to follow.

We dedicate this book to God's perfect and complete will for our marriage. We believe that our marriage IS our ministry and we will continue to trust God for direction and guidance for all that we do for His kingdom. We honestly hope that every couple that reads this book will find some reason to lean closer together and trust God for brighter and more enjoyable days.

It is the mission and vision of Pastor Chef to give couples greater reason to spend more quality time together. It has never been about the food (even though the food is AMAZING).

Contents

INTRODUCTION

Pastor Chefs – We are NOT chefs; we are just two pastors that like to cook.

A couple that prays together... reads together... Prays together... and cooks together (will find a way to stay together!)

Can you go a day without complaining? How about two? Well, we challenge you to go twenty-one days without uttering a single complaint. For the next 21 days we challenge you to focus on the things that are right in your relationship without giving any voice to the things that are "less right". If you can make it through the next 21 days, you will see not only a complete transformation in your relationship but quite possibly a complete transformation in your life!

STOP COMPLAINING SO MUCH! STOP WHINING SO MUCH! Don't just try to read this book so you can say you did, instead digest the concept of not complaining, adopt NOT complaining as a lifestyle, and bring this challenge into your marriage and relationship as a daily commitment. As the pastor of a small church, I've noticed that most people complain without even realizing just how destructive their words are to their relationships. They complain about little things with the same energy and passion that they complain about big things. And then they wonder why there is so much tension in their homes and families. They complain about their spouses and then wonder where all the passion went. They complain not realizing that their complaints block their blessings and generate the wrath of God.

> *And the Lord spoke to Moses and Aaron, saying, "**How long shall I bear with this evil congregation who complain against Me?** I have heard the complaints which the children of Israel make against Me. Say to them, 'As I live,' says the Lord, 'just as you have spoken in My hearing, so I will do to you: The carcasses of you who have complained against Me shall fall in this wilderness, all of you who were numbered, according to your entire number, from twenty years old and above. Numbers 14:26-29(KJV)*

God sees people who complain against what he's done for them as "evil" and in the end God punishes the whiners and complainers because of their whining and complaining. Complaints block blessings and bring a curse to the people who commit to this lifestyle of complaints. A healthy marriage and strong relationship has to be built on a foundation of a positive perspective and not the curse generating energy of a negative outlook.

For the next Twenty-one days you will be expected to work hard to hold your-self and your spouse accountable for every idle word of complaint that comes out of your mouth. Just like God does.

> *But I say to you that for every idle word men may speak, they will give account of it in the day of Judgment. Matthew 12:36*

God is going to hold you accountable for every... Idle...Word. Ok, who's ready for that? I'm sure that most people who read this will say they are not ready, be-cause deep down they know that many of the words that come out of our mouth are not worthy of accountability. It's time for a fresh start in how you communicate with the world and with your spouse.

Accepting this challenge will not only change your marriage, but it will also change your home, your connection with your friends, your ministry and your life!

A husband and wife who chose not to complain will create connections in their relationship they never thought possible.

Priority Time

It is our belief that marriages are strengthened when couples commit to giving one another personal uninterrupted time that overrides all of the other issues in their lives. This is time that a spouse "choses" to give in replacement for every other option. We have decided to define this concept as PRIORITY TIME.

PRIORITY TIME is the time spent with your spouse that **overrides** all other issues, concerns or prior time constraints. That means, regardless of how you feel or what's on your schedule, you choose to make time with your spouse your TOP PRIORITY. For the duration for this challenge once accepted you agree that your PRIORITY TIME ASSIGNMENTS MUST be completed before you close your eyes for the night. (In other words, no matter how late or how dark or how tired you may be... you agree that nothing will take PRIORITY over your spouse and your commitment to see this challenge through... without complaining!)

We know a lot of couples that are going through the ringer right now, some who are convinced they've tried everything possible to save their relationship, a few who are simply believing God for a miracle. And others who now exist on that unfortunate treadmill of **pretending** to be happy in public while in private they live and feel deeply miserable and alone. It is our contention that if you give 21 days of DEDICATED and PRIORITY effort into your relationship, you will see returns come back to you in ways you never expected or believed were even possible. SOMETIMES YOU JUST HAVE TO TRUST GOD with your relationship.

This book is a challenge to every married couple that feels the need and the desire to connect or reconnect with one another. This is a challenge to set aside your own personal time and your personal activities for PRIORITY TIME with your spouse.

Stop Whining... Stop Complaining

NO Venting, Gossiping, Whining, "Explaining," "stating a fact," that is absolutely no complaining at all...NO NONE AT ALL!!!!! Ok, did we get your attention? Marriage is complicated and hard enough without giving power to the areas in your relationship where you and your spouse are unhappy. Death and life are in the power of your words. Death and life are in the power of your idle conversation. The death or the life of your relationship are in the words you choose. Your words will determine the atmosphere you choose to live in. We are challenging you to eliminate negativity from your conversation and replace it with praise. This challenge will help your count your blessings instead of your issues. It's time to move your relationship on a new more positive track.

> *Do all things without grumbling or questioning. Philippians 2:14*

> *Let no corrupting talk come out of your mouths, but only such as is good for building up, as fits the occasion, that it may give grace to those who hear. Ephesians 4:29*

> *Do not grumble against one another, brothers, so that you may not be judged; behold, the Judge is standing at the door. James 5:9*

NO GRUMBLING... NO QUESTIONINGS... NO CORRUPT CHATTER... NO BEING THE ONE THAT HAS TO "TELL IT LIKE IT IS."

This 21-day challenge will bring tremendous awareness to how you think about your marriage and your spouse. Just by attempting to remaining 100% positive with your words will open your eyes to the negative tendencies that you have allowed to take root and gain power over your thoughts, emotions and relationship.

The goal of this challenge is not simply to create a single new success habit for your relationship. The goal is to fully transform your awareness and to refresh your perspective. Make no mistake, not complaining for 21 days will be difficult and will be a REAL CHALLENGE. We are asking each couple to bring 100% effort, not perfect results. It will be in the mistakes that most of the real insights and revelations will be buried. So bring on the slips and falls, that's how you will learn and grow over the 21 days you spend together.

I don't know about you, but I am tired of stealing my own joy, and the joy of those around me with my grumbling. It's time to stop and I CHALLENGE YOU to join me for 21 days of no complaining, grumbling or gossiping.

If you're ready to take your relationship to a whole new level of positive energy and emotion than BRACE YOURSELF BECAUSE A WORLD OF NO COMPLAINING WILL CHANGE EVERYTHING!

21 Day *No* Complaining Marriage Challenge

Pastor Chefs 21 Day No Complaining Marriage Challenge

If you complete the challenges for all 21 days, you will notice a closer connection with your spouse, you will be better able to handle the stressors associated with being in a relationship by learning to press through them WITHOUT complaining, and you will enjoy AMAZING dishes that you cook together. You will enjoy a closer connection with your spouse as well as a more positive and peaceful home.

If you and your spouse accept this challenge, here's what you will need to do:

- Be willing to put off making any major relationship decisions (as in should I stay or leave the relationship) for at least 4 to 6 months. (once the 21 days are complete, allow your new attitude and new routines to set in and transform your relationship)

- Start taking an honest look at yourself as well as your relationship. (Any improvement in your relationship will always start with you).

- Make each day with your spouse and the completion of each challenge your most important priority for that day. (**PRIORITY TIME**).

- Prayerfully work through each challenge. If you are able, record yourselves cooking and watch it later. (this is more fun than you would think)

- Yes, it is important that BOTH spouses participate. This challenge is designed to bring you closer to your spouse by using BOTH of your desires to reconnect and re-energize your relationship.

- **Don't quit!** You WILL want to quit because there will be times that it is just not convenient to complete a day's challenge. **DO IT ANYWAY**. If your marriage is the priority, then press through without regard to convenience.

THIS IS A NO COMPLAINING CHALLENGE! For the next 21 days you agree to:

- Refrain from any negative comments: speak positive and think positively about our self, family, friends, neighbors and others.

- COMPLAIN ABOUT NOTHING: be complimentary about everything and everybody.

- Look for what is good in everything.

- Ask God for a transformation (Romans 12:1-2).

- Don't let your frustration or your realization of the difficulty of this challenge drive you to quit, or to complain. (Don't complain about complaining!)

- For couples make it a point to hold your spouse accountable to the challenge.

I know that someone is reading this and asking the big question; if I can't complain then what DO I do? Complaining has become such a dramatic habit that most people don't even realize just how much they complain, let alone consider an alternative to the constant whining that's become an active part of our normal communication from day today. Instead of complaining you can:

- BE QUIET. Be quiet. Be quiet. And if that doesn't work, be quiet some more. Smile, even if it hurts your face. (Sometimes it will)

- Find something better to do with your energy like checking in on a friend who is struggling or serving others in your community.

- Give thanks! Praise God! Count your blessings! Pray about it. Write it down. Pray some more. Pray with your spouse. Pray over your spouse.

- Confront the problem (if it's worth discussing, it's worth confronting.)

This book will give you an opportunity to begin a journey of gratitude for your relationship, not grumbling to the Lord about what you want or what you don't have in your marriage but instead, offering the Lord a heart of love for the things in your marriage that bring your joy, or the things about your spouse that fill you with peace and commitment.

How to Use this Book

This book is designed to be used as a daily tool to keep your mind focused on something other than issues and other normal daily events that seem worthy of complaining about. This book will be full of quick mind-set shifts/focuses/meditations/devotions and prayers designed to re-train your mind to walk into a new life where complaints don't rule your thinking.

Each day of the challenge set aside time for discussion and conversation with your spouse. Answer all the questions. Make up a few of your own. The goal is for you and your spouse to begin to enjoy one another's company and reconnect in ways you haven't in some times. Use this time to replace your natural urge to complain.

A conscious mind set requires regular and scheduled practice. Unfortunately, you've heard and processed so much negative messaging that it's become the norm of your regular and everyday thinking. Whether you realize it or not, 21 days of not complaining IS POSSIBLE if you feed your mind positivity every single day along the way.

There is power in repetition. There is power in living a synchronistic and predicable life. There is power in a life full of habits that lead to the power of positively trusting God and not giving voice to the negative things you don't even want. It's time to take back you power and your voice, at the end of this 21 days your conversation and your thinking will not and will NEVER again be the same.

Remember this is a Marriage and/or Relationship Challenge, you will NEED an accountability partner to get the most out of this challenge. This challenge is not designed to build and strengthen you alone, but to strengthen your entire relationship. Give it all you have and watch God create connections and open doors in your relationship that you've never thought could be opened. There is real power in giving priority time to your relationship.

21 DAY MARRIAGE CHALLENGE:

- PRIORITIZE daily prayer and devotion WITH your spouse (NOT ALONE…EVER).

- PRAY together, touching and agreeing for God to move in your family.

- DISCUSS daily topics ALL DAY LONG (You can do it if you REALLY try)

- READ prescribed scriptures to one another (NOT alone or apart)

- KEEP a praise journal (write down the areas where you were blessed each and every day)

- COUNT your blessings (literally… how many times were you blessed that day)

- COOK together following the recipes TO THE LETTER. (this will be you reward)

- At the end of each day REFLECT on the challenge and how you FEEL about what you did that day.

- Discuss the challenge of not complaining each and every day. Hold one another accountable to this effort.

Just in case you forgot:
PRIORITY TIME: Time spent with your spouse that OVERRIDES all other issues and concerns. That means, regardless of how you feel or what's on your schedule, your PRIORITY TIME ASSIGNMENT MUST be completed before you close your eyes for the night.

Are you ready to accept this challenge?

21 Day Covenant Agreement

Please Sign and Agree:

Our Commitment
I commit to completing this 21-day challenge with prayer and with honesty. I will do my best to complete all 21 daily assignments, devotions and discussions. I commit to being faithful and honest with my spouse throughout this process. I commit to giving my relationship PRIORITY TIME within each challenge activity. I will make certain that this process remains at the top of my priority list and schedule, and when the process is difficult, I will press on. **As of this moment, my spouse is my TOP PRIORITY.**

I agree and accept that Priority Time will be defined as time spent with your spouse that OVERRIDES all other issues and concerns. That means, regardless of how I feel or what's on my schedule, my PRIORITY TIME ASSIGNMENT MUST be completed before I close my eyes for the night.

For twenty-one (21) days we agree to **pray together, read together, cook together** *and* **hold one another accountable** *to the concept of not complaining and commit to being providing only positive words and energy over our relationship. At the end of each day we will make a personal marriage declaration over our family. We do not expect this to be easy, but we do expect and commit to doing this together!*

I understand this pledge is a reflection of my commitment to this relationship.

_____ *Date* _____

_____ *Date* _____

What do you think will be the hardest part of this challenge?

What do you think will be the hardest part of this challenge for your spouse?

Pray together:

Lord, thank you for giving me the courage to accept this challenge for my marriage. I am thanking You in advance for giving me the strength to see this through to the very end. I have made up my mind today, that my marriage is important enough for me to give it priority over my job, my friends, my hobbies, or any other worldly concerns. In Jesus' name I surrender my own efforts and my own goals to You and commit to giving PRIORITY TIME to You Lord and to my Marriage. I will be grateful for the life You have given me and the relationship You have placed me within. I will praise you and rejoice before you, I will NOT complain. I accept this challenge in Jesus' name. Amen.

CHALLENGE ACCEPTED

CHALLENGE DAY ONE

Challenge Day One Declaration

Can You Remember Why You God Married in the First Place?

Finally, brothers, whatever is true, whatever is noble, whatever is right, whatever is pure, whatever is lovely, whatever is admirable--if anything is excellent or praiseworthy--think about such things. Philippians 4:8

TODAY, I will practice walking in the confidence that my life and the life of my family is moving in the right direction. TODAY I will practice walking in the confidence that come from being clear that we are moving into a time like no other time in our lives. TODAY I make up my mind to START living without complaint nor frustration. TODAY, I have made up my mind to live free from fear and function fully persuaded that God is with me and my family.

Today, we will not complain.

DISCUSSION TOPIC
(Pray before each discussion that God will bring back the best memories)

Do you remember the EXACT reason you got married? Do you remember the EXACT reason you said I do? Ask your spouse specific question about your very first thoughts of marriage. Marriage gets harder when you forget why you married your spouse in the first place. The prevailing thought is that people change or you didn't really know them when you married them, but we would like to suggest that you think back on those first days and reimagine those thoughts and those feelings....

Happiness is a decision. Joy is a choice. With every sunrise, you have a reason and an opportunity to take the alternative path to gratitude for all that God has done. With the hectic and complicated lives that most couples live today and the constant stream of negative news that fills the atmosphere, it's easy to see how a couple could fail to notice the wonderful thing in their lives worth praising over. Do you spend more energy complaining about the blessings you want but don't have that you can barely notice let alone appreciate the blessings that you do have? Stop. Slow down. **Take a deep breath and look around, let today be the day you start counting blessings and stop naming curses over your relationship.**

DAILY PRAYER

Before you get out of the bed, before you brush your teeth, before you do anything that is a normal part of your morning routine. Turn to your spouse, don't sit up and don't get up, simply turn over and pray. Ask God to be an active part of your morning. Ask God to give you the strength to make early Morning Prayer a normal part of your life and relationship. Ask God to help you take control of your words. Touch and agree that you and your spouse can go the entire first day without a single complaint. The first day is always the hardest day, you may need to agree to call one another during the course of the day to pray.

Day one prayer: anoint one another with your oil and love. Ask God to give you the strength you will need not to complain about your spouse for the next 21-days!

MARRIAGE CHALLENGE

Are you willing to do whatever it takes to spend quality and priority time with your spouse? Are you willing to commit more positive energy to your relationship than negative? Do you commit to giving 21 days of NO COMPLAINING for your relationship? Write down your plan, be specific.

Remember to follow this recipe to the letter. It's not about the meal; it's about the *priority time* that you spend together.

No complaining, not whining, just enjoy your time with one another.

Pastor Chefs Mirin-Poached Salmon with Spring Salad

Ingredients

1/3 cup water
3 tablespoons mirin (see Tips)
3 tablespoons reduced-sodium soy sauce
1 tablespoon white vinegar
2 tablespoons fresh ginger matchsticks (see Tips)
1 prayer of agreement
1/4 pounds' salmon, tuna, mahi-mahi or cod, skinned if desired, cut into 4 portions
1/4 teaspoon salt
1 cup radish matchsticks
1 cup thinly sliced snap peas
1 cup pea sprouts

Preparation

Combine water, mirin, soy sauce, vinegar and ginger in a large skillet. Bring to a boil over medium-high heat. Cook for 4 minutes. Add fish; sprinkle with salt. Cover, reduce heat to medium and cook, turning once, just until opaque in the center, 4 to 8 minutes (depending on thickness).

Meanwhile add the prayer of agreement (stop hold hands and pray), then combine radishes, snap peas and pea sprouts in a medium bowl. When the fish is done, pour the braising liquid into the bowl and toss to coat. Serve the salad on the fish.

Before you sit down to enjoy your absolutely perfect steak, give your spouse the most gentle and emotionally tender kiss you can generate. Don't Complain.

Day One Challenge Reflection

The Pastor Chef NO COMPLAINING Challenge is 21 days of PRAYING together, DISCUSSING daily topics, READING together, COOKING together and Holding one another ACCOUNTABLE to the concept of not complaining. Then close the day with a FAMILY DECLARATION!!!

It's not enough for couples to just stop complain, couples need to master counting their blessings **as a couple** from day to day.

HOW TO COUNT YOUR DAILY BLESSINGS

Below are three simple ways to count your blessings as a couple every day:

1) **Journal your blessings all through the day.** Rather than saving your gratitude journal activities for bedtime only, why not make them an ongoing activity all day long? **Keep a small notebook and pencil in your pocket and <u>write a quick note every time something positive happens</u>.**

Little things matter! The more you focus on them, the more you'll begin to feel grateful about the bigger things too. Be prepared to share every positive experience with your spouse.

Quick List for your daily Discussion: (you may need more paper) _____

_____

_____

_____

_____

_____

_____

2) Just like you can journal your positive experiences, you can make it your mission to find something positive about difficult situations. <u>Using the same little notebook,</u> **every time you encounter a challenge or seemingly negative situation, find at least one positive thing you can say about it and write it down**. (at least try)

Quick List for your daily Discussion: _____

_____

_____

_____

_____

3) Finally, you could **literally count your blessings**. Rather than recording the specifics, **simply make a mark in your notebook** every time you experience something to feel grateful about. At the end of the day, glance over your page of marks. How many are there? Make a note of the number and then try to beat it each day afterwards. There are literally thousands of possible things to be grateful about in the course of a single day; you just have to be willing to see them.

How many marks are in your notebook? _____

(share with your spouse).

CHALLENGE DAY ONE COMPLETE

Challenge Day Two Declaration

TODAY, I am a brand new creature, I am a brand new man. I am not afraid to start over and pursue my dreams. TODAY, I declare that I am NOT afraid and I am willing to give myself and my relationship another chance to have all of the things I dreamed of for my family to come true. TODAY, I am a winner and not a loser. TODAY, I personally represent the head and not the tail. TODAY, I refuse to let my mistakes and weaknesses nor any event in my past have power over my life!

Today, we will not complain.

CHALLENGE DAY TWO

Do Remember Your First Date?

Do all things without murmurings and disputing. Philippians 2:14

DISCUSSION TOPIC
(Pray before each discussion that God will bring back the best memories)

What did you do on your first date? What was your favorite part of the date? Did you know on your first date that you were going to marry your spouse? (do you think they knew) Did you expect for there to be a second date? What did you talk about on your first date? What did you laugh about?

Did you know that the bible offers a garment of praise for the spirit of heaviness? So when you put on this garment of Praise, that spirit of heaviness has to go. You won't always feel like having a good attitude. You won't always feel like being grateful for your life. That is why God said to offer up praise as a sacrifice. God knew it would not always be easy. Sometimes you have to dig down deep and say, "God, I don't feel like doing this. It doesn't look like this is going to work out. I'm tired, lonely, discouraged. But Lord, I know You're still on the throne. I know You are good and You are good all the time so I choose to give You praise. I choose to give you thanks instead of constantly complaining about things only You can change. I trust You Lord, and I WILL NOT COMPLAIN!"

DAILY PRAYER

Before you start your day, before you leave your room in the morning hold hands and PRAY (read together and then add your own words of love and support for your spouse):

Father, I am so grateful for Your blessings in my life and am also so very grateful for the spouse that You have given to me. I am grateful that you have enabled me be a blessing to the people that I love. Help me to be more connected to my spouse today and help me to focus on adding to his/her life with encouragement and prayer. Amen.

MARRIAGE CHALLENGE

Relive the first date. Go to the same place or a similar place. Try to have the EX-ACT same conversation... Have this very serious, fun and emotional conversation without complaining.

Remember to follow this recipe to the letter. It's not about the meal; it's about the *priority time* that you spend together.

No complaining, not whining, just enjoy your time with one another.

Pastor Chefs Spaghetti Genovese

Ingredients

2 cups packed baby spinach
8 ounces' whole-wheat spaghetti
1 cup thinly sliced new or baby potatoes (about 4 ounces)
2 words of encouragement
1 pound green beans, trimmed and cut into 1-inch pieces
1/2 cup prepared pesto
1 teaspoon freshly ground pepper
1/2 teaspoon salt

Preparation

Before you begin cooking, give your spouse one word of encouragement. Bring a large pot of water to a boil over medium-high heat. Add spinach and cook just until wilted, about 45 seconds. Use a slotted spoon or fine sieve to transfer the spinach to a blender. Return the water to a boil and add spaghetti and potatoes. Cook, stirring once or twice, until almost tender, 6 to 7 minutes. Add green beans and cook until tender, 3 to 4 minutes more.

When the spaghetti and vegetables are almost done, carefully scoop out 1 cup of the cooking liquid from the pot. Pour 1/2 cup of the liquid into the blender and add pesto, pepper and salt. Blend until smooth, stopping to scrape down the sides as necessary.

Drain the spaghetti and vegetables and return to the pot; stir in the pesto mixture. Cook over medium heat, stirring gently, until the sauce is thickened and the pasta is hot, 1 to 2 minutes. Add more of the cooking liquid, as desired, for a thinner sauce.

Before you sit down to eat, give your spouse another word of encouragement

Day Two Challenge Reflection

The Pastor Chef NO COMPLAINING Challenge is 21 days of PRAYING together, DISCUSSING daily topics, READING together, COOKING together and Holding one another ACCOUNTABLE to the concept of not complaining. Then close the day with a FAMILY DECLARATION!!!

It's not enough for couples to just stop complain, couples need to master counting their blessings **as a couple** from day to day.

HOW TO COUNT YOUR DAILY BLESSINGS

Below are three simple ways to count your blessings as a couple every day:

1) **Journal your blessings all through the day.** Rather than saving your gratitude journal activities for bedtime only, why not make them an ongoing activity all day long? **Keep a small notebook and pencil in your pocket and <u>write a quick note every time something positive happens</u>.**

Little things matter! The more you focus on them, the more you'll begin to feel grateful about the bigger things too. Be prepared to share every positive experience with your spouse.

Quick List for your daily Discussion: (you may need more paper) _____

_____

_____

_____

_____

_____

_____

_____

2) Just like you can journal your positive experiences, you can make it your mission to find something positive about difficult situations. Using the same little notebook, **every time you encounter a challenge or seemingly negative situation, find at least one positive thing you can say about it and write it down**. (at least try)

Quick List for your daily Discussion: _____

_____

_____

_____

_____

3) Finally, you could **literally count your blessings**. Rather than recording the specifics, **simply make a mark in your notebook** every time you experience something to feel grateful about. At the end of the day, glance over your page of marks. How many are there? Make a note of the number and then try to beat it each day afterwards. There are literally thousands of possible things to be grateful about in the course of a single day; you just have to be willing to see them.

How many marks are in your notebook? _____

(share with your spouse).

CHALLENGE DAY TWO COMPLETE

Challenge Day Three Declaration

TODAY, I practice receiving from God in every area in my life. I do not and will not reject any conversation with my spouse nor any Word that comes from the Lord. I will pay attention to God's love, joy, peace and grace that has been seeded in every encounter throughout my day. TODAY, I commit to speak only words that reflect that same life, love, joy, peace and grace into the atmosphere and declare only positive energy into my relationship. Everything comes alive in my presence as I am present to be alive in my relationship.

Today, we will not complain.

CHALLENGE DAY THREE

Do You Remember the First Time you Saw Your Spouse? (first impression)

Let no corrupt communication proceed out of your mouth, but that which is good to the use of edifying, that it may minister grace unto the hearers. Ephesians 4:29

DISCUSSION TOPIC
(Pray before each discussion that God will bring back the best memories)

Tell the story, when was the very first time you laid eyes upon your spouse? What was your first impression? What were they wearing? What were YOU wearing? Did you think you would go out with this person? (Did you know you would marry this person?) How long after the first meeting did you ask your spouse on a date? (who asked whom) How long did it take for you to realize you wanted to marry your spouse?

It is important that you realize that every single day in your relationship is a gift from God, even the very first. Once this day is gone, we can never retrieve it. If we make the mistake of being negative, discouraged, grumpy, sour or spend the entire day complaining, we've wasted the day. Some people squander year after year after year, being unhappy because somebody is not treating them right, or because they are not getting their way, or because their plans are not working out as quickly as they would like. I've made up my mind to not waste any more days in my relationship. I'm celebrating each and every moment with my spouse as a gift from God.

DAILY PRAYER

Before you start your day, before you leave your room in the morning hold hands and PRAY (read together and then add your own words of love and support for your spouse):

Father, I am so thankful that you love me and You have given me an ability to love others. I am so thankful that you have given me a person to love and to cherish and who will love and cherish me in return. Let Your love flow through us today in ways that will be a blessing to others and set an example of what true love can be. Thank you, Lord. Amen.

MARRIAGE CHALLENGE

What will be the biggest challenge of keeping your spouse accountable to not complaining during this challenge? Develop a strategy to overcome that issue. Have this discussion without complaining.   We challenge you to go sit in the back seat of your car and make out. (if you don't have a car... pretend)

Remember to follow this recipe to the letter. It's not about the meal; it's about the *priority time* that you spend together.

No complaining, not whining, just enjoy your time with one another.

Pastor Chefs Zesty Shrimp & Black Bean Salad

Ingredients

1/4 cup cider vinegar
3 tablespoons extra-virgin olive oil
1 tablespoon minced chipotle chile in adobo (see Tips), or more to taste
1 teaspoon ground cumin
1/4 teaspoon salt
1 pound peeled and deveined cooked shrimp (see Tips), cut into 1/2-inch pieces
1 15-ounce can black beans, rinsed
1 tight hug
1 cup quartered cherry tomatoes
1 large poblano pepper or bell pepper, chopped
1/4 cup chopped scallions
1 Full Kiss
1/4 cup chopped fresh cilantro

Preparation

Whisk vinegar, oil, chipotle, cumin and salt in a large bowl. Add a tight hug, shrimp, beans, tomatoes, poblano (or bell pepper), scallions and cilantro; toss to coat. Serve room temperature or cold. Add some heat with 1 Full Kiss before serving.

Tips & Notes

Make Ahead Tip: Cover and refrigerate for up to 1 day.

Tips: Peppers, chipotle, in adobo sauce: Chipotle chiles in adobo sauce are smoked jalapeños packed in a flavorful sauce. Look for the small cans with Mexican foods at large supermarkets. Once opened, they'll keep up to 2 weeks in the refrigerator or 6 months in the freezer.

To peel, grasp the legs and hold onto the tail while you twist off the shell. To devein, use a paring knife to make a slit along the length of the shrimp. Remove the dark digestive tract (or "vein") with the knife tip.

Have you ever had your spouse feed you an entire meal? We challenge you to start with this one. Feed your spouse entire plate; make it fun! No complaining!

Day Three Challenge Reflection

The Pastor Chef NO COMPLAINING Challenge is 21 days of PRAYING together, DISCUSSING daily topics, READING together, COOKING together and Holding one another ACCOUNTABLE to the concept of not complaining. Then close the day with a FAMILY DECLARATION!!!

It's not enough for couples to just stop complain, couples need to master counting their blessings **as a couple** from day to day.

HOW TO COUNT YOUR DAILY BLESSINGS

Below are three simple ways to count your blessings as a couple every day:

1) **Journal your blessings all through the day.** Rather than saving your gratitude journal activities for bedtime only, why not make them an ongoing activity all day long? **Keep a small notebook and pencil in your pocket and <u>write a quick note every time something positive happens</u>.**

Little things matter! The more you focus on them, the more you'll begin to feel grateful about the bigger things too. Be prepared to share every positive experience with your spouse.

Quick List for your daily Discussion: (you may need more paper) _____

_____

_____

_____

_____

_____

_____

_____

2) Just like you can journal your positive experiences, you can make it your mission to find something positive about difficult situations. <u>Using the same little notebook</u>, **every time you encounter a challenge or seemingly negative situation, find at least one positive thing you can say about it and write it down**. (at least try)

Quick List for your daily Discussion: _____

_____

_____

_____

_____

3) Finally, you could **literally count your blessings**. Rather than recording the specifics, **simply make a mark in your notebook** every time you experience something to feel grateful about. At the end of the day, glance over your page of marks. How many are there? Make a note of the number and then try to beat it each day afterwards. There are literally thousands of possible things to be grateful about in the course of a single day; you just have to be willing to see them.

How many marks are in your notebook? _____
(share with your spouse).

CHALLENGE DAY THREE COMPLETE

Challenge Day Four Declaration

CHALLENGE DAY FOUR

Do You Remember Your First Kiss?

In everything give thanks: for this is the will of God in Christ Jesus concerning you. 1 Thessalonians 5:18

DISCUSSION TOPIC
(Pray before each discussion that God will bring back the best memories)

TODAY, I DECLARE TO THE WORLD that I have a good marriage. I declare that I will make the most of this relationship and that we will live out all of our dreams together. I am convinced that God has a plan for my marriage and I will enjoy my spouse to the fullest knowing that God will honor and bless our connection. I declare to the world and to my spouse that we will live and love and not miss out on the best parts of our lives together. And we will start TODAY!

Today, we will not complain.

Do you remember your fist kiss? Was it romantic or was it awkward? Do you remember the first time you held hands? Did you talk about the kiss? Did you think about it the next day? Do you remember the first time romantic conversation that led to a kiss?

You may not realize it but God has already given you everything you need to be happy. He has given you ever moment for joy and happiness. God has placed in your spouse every moment worth living and a partner suitable for victory again any enemy. You don't need a big house or the latest car to find joy in your relationship. What you need is a fresh and clear perspective. Seeing your relationship, the way God wants you to see your relationship is the first step in shutting the door to whining and complaining.

DAILY PRAYER

Before you start your day, before you leave your room in the morning hold hands and PRAY (read together and then add your own words of love and support for your spouse):
We thank you, Father, that we can boldly declare in faith who we are and who we represent in Christ. Thank You that You created us as a one of a kind relationship. Thank You for a complete and satisfying love in my spouse and in our relationship. Today we choose to believe and trust God that we God's perfect and specific workmanship. Created for His glory and to bring praise to His name. AMEN

MARRIAGE CHALLENGE

24 Hours NO SCREENS AT ALL WITHOUT WHINING.
(NO TV, NO COMPUTERS, NO TABLETS, NO CELL PHONES, NO SOCIAL
MEDIA) Give all of your time to your spouse for 24 hours (this is priority time...
you may have to do this on a weekend day)

Remember to follow this recipe to the letter. It's not about the meal; it's about the *priority time* that you spend together.

No complaining, not whining, just enjoy your time with one another.

Pastor Chefs Tilapia with Tomato-Olive Sauce

Ingredients

1 1/4 pounds tilapia
1/4 teaspoon salt
1/4 teaspoon freshly ground pepper
2 tablespoons extra-virgin olive oil, divided
1 pint grape or cherry tomatoes, halved if large
1/4 cup dry white wine
2 passionate kisses
3 cloves garlic, finely chopped
3 tablespoons olive tapenade

Preparation

Sprinkle tilapia with salt and pepper. Heat 1 tablespoon oil in a large nonstick skillet over medium-high heat. Add the fish and cook (in two batches if necessary), turning once halfway through, until golden brown and just opaque in the center, 4 to 6 minutes' total. Add one passionate kiss, transfer the fish to a serving platter; tent with foil to keep warm.

Off the heat, add the remaining 1 tablespoon oil, tomatoes, wine and garlic to the pan. Return to medium heat, cover and cook, stirring occasionally, this is a good place to give your spouse a little sugar, add another passion kiss until most of tomatoes are broken down, 4 to 5 minutes. Stir in olive tapenade and cook for 1 minute more. Serve the fish with the sauce.

Dim the lights and passionately look into each other's eyes over your meal. (Don't stop passionately looking into each other's eyes until your entire meal is gone... it's ok to giggle) Have Fun with this one. No complaining!

Day Four Challenge Reflection

The Pastor Chef NO COMPLAINING Challenge is 21 days of PRAYING together, DISCUSSING daily topics, READING together, COOKING together and Holding one another ACCOUNTABLE to the concept of not complaining. Then close the day with a FAMILY DECLARATION!!!

It's not enough for couples to just stop complain, couples need to master counting their blessings **as a couple** from day to day.

HOW TO COUNT YOUR DAILY BLESSINGS

Below are three simple ways to count your blessings as a couple every day:

1) **Journal your blessings all through the day.** Rather than saving your gratitude journal activities for bedtime only, why not make them an ongoing activity all day long? **Keep a small notebook and pencil in your pocket and <u>write a quick note every time something positive happens</u>.**

Little things matter! The more you focus on them, the more you'll begin to feel grateful about the bigger things too. Be prepared to share every positive experience with your spouse.

Quick List for your daily Discussion: (you may need more paper) _____

_____

_____

_____

_____

_____

_____

2) Just like you can journal your positive experiences, you can make it your mission to find something positive about difficult situations. Using the same little notebook, **every time you encounter a challenge or seemingly negative situation, find at least one positive thing you can say about it and write it down**. (at least try)

Quick List for your daily Discussion: _____

_____

_____

_____

_____

3) Finally, you could **literally count your blessings**. Rather than recording the specifics, **simply make a mark in your notebook** every time you experience something to feel grateful about. At the end of the day, glance over your page of marks. How many are there? Make a note of the number and then try to beat it each day afterwards. There are literally thousands of possible things to be grateful about in the course of a single day; you just have to be willing to see them.

How many marks are in your notebook? _____

(share with your spouse).

CHALLENGE DAY FOUR COMPLETE

Challenge Day Five Declaration

TODAY, I declare victory in my relationship and bind any spiritual attack from over the relationship I have with my spouse. I have made up my mind that I will pray more, study more and work harder to become more spiritually connected to my spouse. I declare that I will not give when things get hard but surrender be more willing to surrender the results to the God I believe in. I have made up my mind that I will trust God, even when things get hard.

Today, we will not complain.

CHALLENGE DAY FIVE

Have You Discussed Your Legacy?

Every place that the sole of your foot will tread upon I have given you, as I said to Moses. Joshua 1:3

DISCUSSION TOPIC
(Pray before each discussion that God will bring back the best memories)

No one lives forever, have you and your spouse had an opportunity to discuss what you would like the world to think of you when you are gone? Are you and your spouse working on your legacy together or apart? Do you have a long term plan? Do you have a short term plan?

Take a step of faith and no matter how you feel make up your mind that you will agree with God. Combined you and your spouse have been given many talents, gifts and strengths. Isn't it time for you to start using the gifts and talents that God has given to you. Make declarations you're your future and into your family's legacy. Speak words of healing and not words of destruction. Fight for your family! Fight the good fight of faith and refuse to live below the level that God called you to live. His kingdom is righteousness, peace and joy (see Romans 14:17) REFUSE to settle for less.

DAILY PRAYER

Before you start your day, before you leave your room in the morning hold hands and PRAY (read together and then add your own words of love and support for your spouse):

Father, I am so very grateful that I can trust You to help me learn from my mistakes in my marriage. I don't have to worry or be afraid that I'll make the wrong decisions in this relationship, because I know You are with me and will make sure that all things work together for our good. Thank You for leading and guiding us in this marriage – even through our mistakes. AMEN.

MARRIAGE CHALLENGE

Love keeps no record of wrongs... perfect love drives out fear. We challenge you to let go of any mistakes you've been holding against your spouse. This is a test of how strong you are a person... can you let it go? (without complaining, without anger) can you let go? Well? Can you?

Remember to follow this recipe to the letter. It's not about the meal; it's about the *priority time* that you spend together.

No complaining, not whining, just enjoy your time with one another.

Pastor Chefs Seared Salmon with Green Peppercorn Sauce

Ingredients

1 1/4 pounds wild salmon fillet (see Tip), skinned and cut into 4 portions
1/4 teaspoon plus a pinch of salt, divided
2 teaspoons canola oil
1 flirty pickup line
1/4 cup lemon juice
4 teaspoons unsalted butter, cut into small pieces
1 teaspoon green peppercorns in vinegar, rinsed and crushed

Preparation

Sprinkle salmon pieces with 1/4 teaspoon salt. Heat oil in a large nonstick skillet over medium-high heat. Add the salmon and cook until just opaque in the center, gently turning halfway, 4 to 7 minutes total. Divide among 4 plates. Remove the pan from the heat and immediately add lemon juice, butter, peppercorns and the remaining pinch of salt; swirl the pan carefully to incorporate the butter into the sauce. Top each portion of fish with sauce (about 2 teaspoons each). To top it off, add 1 flirty pickup line.

Tips & Notes

Tips: Wild-caught salmon from the Pacific (Alaska and Washington) is considered the best choice for the environment because it is more sustainably fished and has a larger, more stable population. Farmed salmon, including Atlantic, should be avoided, as it endangers the wild salmon population.

To skin salmon, place fillet on a clean cutting board, skin side down. Starting at the tail end, slip the blade of a long, sharp knife between the fish flesh and the skin, holding the skin down firmly with your other hand. Gently push the blade along at a 30° angle, separating the fillet from the skin without cutting through either.

Light some candles, relax and enjoy a romantic dinner with your spouse. Enjoy a complaint free conversation.

Day Five Challenge Reflection

The Pastor Chef NO COMPLAINING Challenge is 21 days of PRAYING together, DISCUSSING daily topics, READING together, COOKING together and Holding one another ACCOUNTABLE to the concept of not complaining. Then close the day with a FAMILY DECLARATION!!!

It's not enough for couples to just stop complain, couples need to master counting their blessings **as a couple** from day to day.

HOW TO COUNT YOUR DAILY BLESSINGS

Below are three simple ways to count your blessings as a couple every day:

1) **Journal your blessings all through the day.** Rather than saving your gratitude journal activities for bedtime only, why not make them an ongoing activity all day long? **Keep a small notebook and pencil in your pocket and <u>write a quick note every time something positive happens</u>.**

Little things matter! The more you focus on them, the more you'll begin to feel grateful about the bigger things too. Be prepared to share every positive experience with your spouse.

Quick List for your daily Discussion: (you may need more paper) _____

_____

_____

_____

_____

_____

_____

2) Just like you can journal your positive experiences, you can make it your mission to find something positive about difficult situations. <u>Using the same little notebook,</u> **every time you encounter a challenge or seemingly negative situation, find at least one positive thing you can say about it and write it down.** (at least try)

Quick List for your daily Discussion: _____

_____

_____

_____

_____

3) Finally, you could **literally count your blessings**. Rather than recording the specifics, **simply make a mark in your notebook** every time you experience something to feel grateful about. At the end of the day, glance over your page of marks. How many are there? Make a note of the number and then try to beat it each day afterwards. There are literally thousands of possible things to be grateful about in the course of a single day; you just have to be willing to see them.

How many marks are in your notebook? _____

(share with your spouse).

CHALLENGE DAY FIVE COMPLETE

Challenge Day Six Declaration

TODAY, I declare that my marriage is blessed and secure in the love that has been planted within both of us. We declare that we have been called to be together for a great purpose. We decree into our relationship peace and prosperity for as long as we commit to facing every issue together. We REFUSE to be broken by any of the issues that confront our relationship and commit to facing each and every issue hand in hand confident that God will be with us! TODAY I choose to recognize that my marriage and my relationship is a gift from a God that Loves me.

Today, we will not complain.

CHALLENGE DAY SIX

What Is Your Fondest Memory In Your Entire Relationship?

Therefore, there is now no condemnation for those who are in Christ Jesus. Romans 8:1

DISCUSSION TOPIC
(Pray before each discussion that God will bring back the best memories)

Whether you've been married 30 years or 3 years there is at least one positive memory that defines your relationship. One memory that brings the clear reminder exactly WHY you married the person you married. What is the memory that makes you smile when no one is in the room? What is the memory that has become that would make you fly if you were in Never Never Land trying desperately to fly? Share this memory with your spouse. Are your favorite memories the same? Enjoy the conversation.

Positive mind (minds full of faith and hope) produce a positive relationship. Negative minds (Minds full of fear and doubt) produce negative relationships. In Matthew 8:13, Jesus the things we want will only be done as we are able to believe. This doesn't mean that you can get EVERYTHING you want just by thinking about it, but we can clearly block progress by keeping our minds in negative places. We encourage you to think positively about your life and your relationship. Think positively about your life and be thankful for the memories and the positive moments that God has brought you in the short time you've been together. Even if you're going through a difficult situation, stand in faith, believe God will bring good out of it. Trust Him... Even if it's hard. He won't let you down.

DAILY PRAYER

Before you start your day, before you leave your room in the morning hold hands and PRAY (read together and then add your own words of love and support for your spouse):

Dear Lord, thank You for another day, that you see the new more positive attitudes in our hearts. We know that You have given us a new "want to" and with Your help, we are going to do our very best to please you with our relationship. We love You, lord, and we thank You for Your grace in our lives. AMEN.

MARRIAGE CHALLENGE

*Share your vision for your marriage from the last challenge day. Pray about it and come to agreement on the vision. Pray in agreement over the vision. There is **Real Power** in a married couple who have found agreement.*

Remember to follow this recipe to the letter. It's not about the meal; it's about the *priority time* that you spend together.

No complaining, not whining, just enjoy your time with one another.

Pastor Chefs Seared Steak with Pan-Roasted Grape & Port Sauce

Ingredients

1/4 pounds boneless strip steak (about 1 inch thick), trimmed
1/2 teaspoon kosher salt, divided
1/4 teaspoon freshly ground pepper
1 tablespoon extra-virgin olive oil plus 1 teaspoon, divided
1 cup seedless red grapes
1/4 cup diced shallot
Read Song of Solomon 1:2
1 1/2 teaspoons all-purpose flour
1/4 cup port wine
1/4 cup reduced-sodium beef broth
1 teaspoon chopped fresh thyme

Preparation

Pat steaks dry and cut into 4 equal portions. Sprinkle with 1/4 teaspoon salt and pepper. Heat 1 tablespoon oil in a large skillet over medium-high heat until very hot, but not smoking. Add the steaks and cook until browned on the bottom, 2 to 4 minutes. Turn over, reduce heat to medium-low and cook to desired doneness, 3 to 5 minutes for medium-rare. Remove the steaks from the pan and set aside, covered with foil.

Wife: Read Song of Solomon 1:2 to your husband, and husband do what the scripture reads.

Heat the remaining 1 teaspoon oil in the pan over medium-low heat. Add grapes and cook, stirring occasionally and pressing down on them with the back of a spoon, until the grapes are brown in spots and mostly broken down, 4 to 6 minutes. Add shallot and cook, stirring, until fragrant, about 1 minute. Sprinkle with flour and stir to coat. Add port, broth, thyme and the remaining 1/4 teaspoon salt. Increase the heat to medium-high and cook, stirring and scraping up any browned bits, until reduced and thickened, 2 to 3 minutes. Serve the steaks with about 3 tablespoons sauce each.

Wife: Read Song of Solomon 1:2 to your husband, and husband do what the scripture reads. (yes I know… you just did this. Do it again)

Day Six Challenge Reflection

The Pastor Chef NO COMPLAINING Challenge is 21 days of PRAYING together, DISCUSSING daily topics, READING together, COOKING together and Holding one another ACCOUNTABLE to the concept of not complaining. Then close the day with a FAMILY DECLARATION!!!

It's not enough for couples to just stop complain, couples need to master counting their blessings **as a couple** from day to day.

HOW TO COUNT YOUR DAILY BLESSINGS

Below are three simple ways to count your blessings as a couple every day:

1) **Journal your blessings all through the day.** Rather than saving your gratitude journal activities for bedtime only, why not make them an ongoing activity all day long? **Keep a small notebook and pencil in your pocket and <u>write a quick note every time something positive happens</u>.**

Little things matter! The more you focus on them, the more you'll begin to feel grateful about the bigger things too. Be prepared to share every positive experience with your spouse.

Quick List for your daily Discussion: (you may need more paper) _____

_____

_____

_____

_____

_____

_____

_____

2) Just like you can journal your positive experiences, you can make it your mission to find something positive about difficult situations. Using the same little notebook, **every time you encounter a challenge or seemingly negative situation, find at least one positive thing you can say about it and write it down**. (at least try)

Quick List for your daily Discussion: _____

_____

_____

_____

_____

3) Finally, you could **literally count your blessings**. Rather than recording the specifics, **simply make a mark in your notebook** every time you experience something to feel grateful about. At the end of the day, glance over your page of marks. How many are there? Make a note of the number and then try to beat it each day afterwards. There are literally thousands of possible things to be grateful about in the course of a single day; you just have to be willing to see them.

How many marks are in your notebook? _____

(share with your spouse).

CHALLENGE DAY SIX COMPLETE

Challenge Day Seven Declaration

TODAY we declare and speak into the atmosphere peace and blessings over our marriage and over the lives of our children. We declare and decree a restoration of peace and emotional tranquility in our home and bind any spirit that attempts to rob our family of the peace we deserve and desire. The Lord shall be the shield over our family and the sword that we will use to defend our future. Today we declare in agreement that God is in charge of our relationship and we trust Him.

Today, we will not complain.

Do You Remember Your First Christmas (Holiday) Together?

Rejoice in the Lord always. I will say it again: Rejoice!
Philippians 4:4

DISCUSSION TOPIC
(Pray before each discussion that God will bring back the best memories)

Do you remember your first holiday together? Do you remember the first Christmas gift you bought your spouse? Have you ever made a gift for your spouse? (if not make one) Do you remember your first holiday meal? What was your first holiday vacation? What has been your favorite holiday as a married couple? (why?) What was your favorite holiday as a child? Do you have a favorite holiday movie (song)?

There are so many extremely serious things going on in this world, and we need to be aware of them and prepared for them. But at the same time, because of the spirit of God in our lives, we can learn to relax and take things as they come without getting nervous and upset about things not going our way. Thankfully with God's help, we can learn to enjoy the peace and joy God has assigned for our marriage and relationship. In spite of all the difficult and troubling things going on in life, but thankfully God allows us positive memories and purpose and freedom to declare, "This is the day that the Lord has made; I will rejoice and be glad in it."

DAILY PRAYER

Before you start your day, before you leave your room in the morning hold hands and PRAY (read together and then add your own words of love and support for your spouse):
Father, no matter what goes on around us today, we thank You that we can still rejoice and be glad in the relationship that You have given to us. Thank You that our joy is not found in our circumstances but in our confidence in Your name. We have made up our minds that we will find joy in the lives and family that our God has given to us. AMEN.

MARRIAGE CHALLENGE

What is your favorite Christmas song? What is your favorite Christmas movie? We challenge you to sing together (holiday songs). And watch your favorite holiday movie. If you can't agree on the best movie, watch your favorite two (in the same night) having holiday fun together without complaining. (No it doesn't matter if it's the holiday... pretend, besides we celebrate Christmas in January...)

Remember to follow this recipe to the letter. It's not about the meal; it's about the *priority time* that you spend together.

No complaining, not whining, just enjoy your time with one another.

Pastor Chefs Poached Cod & Asparagus

Ingredients

1 lemon, divided
1 cup dry white wine
2 teaspoons cornstarch
1 tablespoon thinly sliced shallot
1 bay leaf
5 whole black peppercorns
1 1/4 pounds cod, cut into 4 equal portions
1/2 teaspoon salt, divided
1/4 teaspoon ground white or black pepper
1 funny joke
4 sprigs fresh tarragon
1 1/2 bunches asparagus (about 1 1/2 pounds), trimmed
1/2 cup water
2 tablespoons butter

Preparation

Juice half the lemon into a small saucepan; reserve the other half. Whisk in wine and cornstarch until combined. Add shallot, bay leaf and peppercorns. Bring to a boil. Reduce heat to maintain a simmer and cook, stirring occasionally, until thickened and reduced by about half, 10 to 12 minutes.

Meanwhile, sprinkle cod with 1/4 teaspoon salt and pepper. Place a tarragon sprig on each portion. Thinly slice the remaining lemon half and lay the slices over the tarragon.

Place asparagus in an even layer in a large skillet. Add 1/2 cup water. Place the cod on top of the asparagus. Bring to a boil over medium heat. Cover and cook until the asparagus is tender and the fish is cooked through, 4 to 5 minutes. Wife: tell your honey a funny joke, and laugh together

Strain the reduced sauce through a sieve into a bowl. Return it to the pan. Over low heat, swirl butter into the sauce 1 tablespoon at a time until melted. Stir in the remaining 1/4 teaspoon salt and remove from the heat.

Serve the fish and asparagus topped with the sauce.

Day Seven Challenge Reflection

The Pastor Chef NO COMPLAINING Challenge is 21 days of PRAYING together, DISCUSSING daily topics, READING together, COOKING together and Holding one another ACCOUNTABLE to the concept of not complaining. Then close the day with a FAMILY DECLARATION!!!

It's not enough for couples to just stop complain, couples need to master counting their blessings **as a couple** from day to day.

HOW TO COUNT YOUR DAILY BLESSINGS

Below are three simple ways to count your blessings as a couple every day:

1) **Journal your blessings all through the day.** Rather than saving your gratitude journal activities for bedtime only, why not make them an ongoing activity all day long? **Keep a small notebook and pencil in your pocket and <u>write a quick note every time something positive happens</u>.**

Little things matter! The more you focus on them, the more you'll begin to feel grateful about the bigger things too. Be prepared to share every positive experience with your spouse.

Quick List for your daily Discussion: (you may need more paper) _____

_____

_____

_____

_____

_____

_____

2) Just like you can journal your positive experiences, you can make it your mission to find something positive about difficult situations. <u>Using the same little notebook</u>, **every time you encounter a challenge or seemingly negative situation, find at least one positive thing you can say about it and write it down**. (at least try)

Quick List for your daily Discussion: _____

_____

_____

_____

_____

3) Finally, you could **literally count your blessings**. Rather than recording the specifics, **simply make a mark in your notebook** every time you experience something to feel grateful about. At the end of the day, glance over your page of marks. How many are there? Make a note of the number and then try to beat it each day afterwards. There are literally thousands of possible things to be grateful about in the course of a single day; you just have to be willing to see them.

How many marks are in your notebook? _____

(share with your spouse).

CHALLENGE DAY SEVEN COMPLETE

Challenge Day Eight Declaration

We declare and decree that God will open doors and abundance into our household. We touch and agree that God will open windows of blessings to flow into our home. To-gether, with God's help and direction, we will accomplish great things in this world. God is moving quickly in and through our lives. Victory is closer than we think, now we declare that in Jesus name we will be ready to achieve great things together! We Trust God together!

Today, we will not complain.

CHALLENGE DAY EIGHT

What is Your Spouse's Best Quality?

The sun has one kind of splendor, the moon another and the stars another; and star differs from star in splendor. 1 Corinthians 15:41

DISCUSSION TOPIC
(Pray before each discussion that God will bring back the best memories)

There is a commercial that comes on from time to time that says "Have you ever had the moment where you look at your spouse and suddenly remember why you married them?" What is your spouse's best quality? What do you think your spouse thinks is your favorite quality? What is your spouse's favorite color? What is the first thing that comes to mind when you think about your spouse? What is the first thing that comes to mind when people think about your spouse?

We are all different. Like the Sun, the moon, and the stars, God has created us to be different from one another, and He has done it on purpose. Each of us meets a need, and we are all part of God's overall plan. God made your spouse perfectly and completely just for you. It's time for each of you to learn to celebrate those differences and not complain about them. Praise God for the difference between you and your spouse. Thankfully we can be secure in ourselves knowing God loves us and has a plan for our relationship. When we struggle to like one another, not only do we lose ourselves, but we also grieve the Holy Spirit. Different is okay; it's alright to be different.

DAILY PRAYER

Before you start your day, before you leave your room in the morning hold hands and PRAY (read together and then add your own words of love and support for your spouse):

Father, You have created us to be distinct and unique, and we thank You and praise You for creating us perfectly and individually. With Your help we will avoid the temptation to compare ourselves to others. We have decided to be secure in who we were created to be TODAY! AMEN.

MARRIAGE CHALLENGE

We challenge you to tell your spouse a story. (no it doesn't matter if it's a long or short story) Now on a scale of one to ten, rate yourself on how well you listen to your spouse? (do you feel like your spouse was listening to your story?) Repeat back your spouse's story.

Pastor Chefs Grilled Salmon with Tomatoes & Basil

CHALLENGE DAY 8

PASTOR CHEFS

RECIPE

(COOK TOGETHER)

Remember to follow this recipe to the letter. It's not about the meal; it's about the *priority time* that you spend together.

No complaining, not whining, just enjoy your time with one another.

Ingredients

2 cloves garlic, minced
1 teaspoon kosher salt, divided
1 tablespoon extra-virgin olive oil
1 thought provoking question
1 whole wild salmon fillet (also called a "side of salmon," about 1 1/2 pounds; see Tips)
1/3 cup plus 1/4 cup thinly sliced fresh basil, divided
2 medium tomatoes, thinly sliced
1/4 teaspoon freshly ground pepper

Preparation

Preheat grill to medium.

Mash minced garlic and 3/4 teaspoon salt on a cutting board with the side of a chef's knife or a spoon until a paste forms. Transfer to a small bowl and stir in oil.

Check the salmon for pin bones and remove if necessary (see Tips). Measure out a piece of heavy-duty foil (or use a double layer of regular foil) large enough for the salmon fillet. Coat the foil with cooking spray. Place the salmon skin-side down on the foil and spread the garlic mixture all over it. Sprinkle with 1/3 cup basil. Overlap tomato slices on top and sprinkle with the remaining 1/4 teaspoon salt and pepper.

Ask each other 1 thought provoking question such as: Are you living your vision (discuss over dinner)

Transfer the salmon on the foil to the grill. Grill until the fish flakes easily, 10 to 12 minutes. Use two large spatulas to slide the salmon from the foil to a serving platter. Serve the salmon sprinkled with the remaining 1/4 cup basil.

Day Eight Challenge Reflection

The Pastor Chef NO COMPLAINING Challenge is 21 days of PRAYING together, DISCUSSING daily topics, READING together, COOKING together and Holding one another ACCOUNTABLE to the concept of not complaining. Then close the day with a FAMILY DECLARATION!!!

It's not enough for couples to just stop complain, couples need to master counting their blessings **as a couple** from day to day.

HOW TO COUNT YOUR DAILY BLESSINGS

Below are three simple ways to count your blessings as a couple every day:

1) **Journal your blessings all through the day.** Rather than saving your gratitude journal activities for bedtime only, why not make them an ongoing activity all day long? **Keep a small notebook and pencil in your pocket and <u>write a quick note every time something positive happens</u>.**

Little things matter! The more you focus on them, the more you'll begin to feel grateful about the bigger things too. Be prepared to share every positive experience with your spouse.

Quick List for your daily Discussion: (you may need more paper) _____

_____

_____

_____

_____

_____

_____

2) Just like you can journal your positive experiences, you can make it your mission to find something positive about difficult situations. Using the same little notebook, **every time you encounter a challenge or seemingly negative situation, find at least one positive thing you can say about it and write it down**. (at least try)

Quick List for your daily Discussion: _____

_____

_____

_____

_____

3) Finally, you could **literally count your blessings**. Rather than recording the specifics, **simply make a mark in your notebook** every time you experience something to feel grateful about. At the end of the day, glance over your page of marks. How many are there? Make a note of the number and then try to beat it each day afterwards. There are literally thousands of possible things to be grateful about in the course of a single day; you just have to be willing to see them.

How many marks are in your notebook? _____
                                         (share with your spouse).

CHALLENGE DAY EIGHT COMPLETE

We declare and decree that God will open a window of heaven's blessings upon our marriage because we are committed to submitting our relationship completely to the Lord. We commit to giving God our passions and our energy. We will strive to see God more clearly manifest himself in our relationship. People will recognize the God in us, because our light will shine so brightly.

Today, we will not complain.

CHALLENGE DAY NINE

Do You Remember Your Thought When You Saw Your Spouse "for the first time" On Your Wedding Day?

For I determined not to know anything among you except Jesus Christ and Him crucified. 1 Corinthians 2:2

DISCUSSION TOPIC
(Pray before each discussion that God will bring back the best memories)

Do you remember the first time you had to tell someone that you were married? Do you remember the first time you saw your spouse and recognized them as your spouse? Do you remember the first conversation you had with someone about being married? What did you wear on your wedding day? What did you wear on your wedding night? Do you think you could fit the clothes you wore when you got married? What would be your fantasy marriage location?

God created you for an exhilarating life that often requires you to take bold leaps of faith. Entering into marriage is a bold leap where in the end, all you can do is trust God with the journey. So many people are unsatisfied with their lives simply because they won't step out or make the choice to step out alone as opposed to sharing that journey with another. They want to stay in a "safe zone" which may feel secure, but is not always where the joy and adventure of life can be found. It may not always be clear or easy to see, but marriage actually is worth the risk. God anointed marriage to allow us to have someone to share the adventure of life.

DAILY PRAYER

Before you start your day, before you leave your room in the morning hold hands and PRAY (read together and then add your own words of love and support for your spouse):

Father, thank You for the example You have set for me and my spouse for our marriage and for our lives. Thank You for the life that you have made possible by the leading of your Spirit. We don't have to live a life full of stress, fear, or worry. Help us to leave those things behind and enjoy the lives You have provided specifically for us. AMEN.

MARRIAGE CHALLENGE

We challenge you to pull out old picture of your wedding and re-live every moment. If you don't have pictures, take some. Either way, take the time to make new memories.

Remember to follow this recipe to the letter. It's not about the meal; it's about the *priority time* that you spend together.

No complaining, not whining, just enjoy your time with one another.

Pastor Chefs Spicy Tunisian Grilled Chicken

Ingredients

2 teaspoons coriander seeds
2 teaspoons caraway seeds
3/4 teaspoon crushed red pepper
3/4 teaspoon garlic powder
2 compliments
1/2 teaspoon kosher salt
1-1 1/4 pounds boneless, skinless chicken breast

Preparation

Wife: give your husband a compliment

Grind coriander seeds, caraway seeds and crushed red pepper in a spice grinder (or mortar and pestle) until finely ground. Transfer to a small bowl and stir in garlic powder and salt.

Coat both sides of chicken with the rub up to 30 minutes before grilling or broiling.

Preheat grill to medium-high or position a rack in upper third of oven and preheat broiler.

To grill: Oil the grill rack (see Tip). Grill the chicken, turning once, until an instant-read thermometer inserted into the thickest part registers 165°F, 4 to 8 minutes per side.

To broil: Line a broiler pan (or baking sheet) with foil and coat with cooking spray. Place the chicken on the foil. Broil, watching carefully and turning at least once, until an instant-read thermometer inserted into the thickest part registers 165°F, 10 to 15 minutes total.

After dinner, wives give your husband another compliment (a sincere compliment that will make him blush)

Day Nine Challenge Reflection

The Pastor Chef NO COMPLAINING Challenge is 21 days of PRAYING together, DISCUSSING daily topics, READING together, COOKING together and Holding one another ACCOUNTABLE to the concept of not complaining. Then close the day with a FAMILY DECLARATION!!!

It's not enough for couples to just stop complain, couples need to master counting their blessings **as a couple** from day to day.

HOW TO COUNT YOUR DAILY BLESSINGS

Below are three simple ways to count your blessings as a couple every day:

1) **Journal your blessings all through the day.** Rather than saving your gratitude journal activities for bedtime only, why not make them an ongoing activity all day long? **Keep a small notebook and pencil in your pocket and <u>write a quick note every time something positive happens</u>.**

Little things matter! The more you focus on them, the more you'll begin to feel grateful about the bigger things too. Be prepared to share every positive experience with your spouse.

Quick List for your daily Discussion: (you may need more paper) _____

_____

_____

_____

_____

_____

_____

2) Just like you can journal your positive experiences, you can make it your mission to find something positive about difficult situations. <u>Using the same little notebook,</u> **every time you encounter a challenge or seemingly negative situation, find at least one positive thing you can say about it and write it down**. (at least try)

Quick List for your daily Discussion: _____

_____

_____

_____

_____

3) Finally, you could **literally count your blessings**. Rather than recording the specifics, **simply make a mark in your notebook** every time you experience something to feel grateful about. At the end of the day, glance over your page of marks. How many are there? Make a note of the number and then try to beat it each day afterwards. There are literally thousands of possible things to be grateful about in the course of a single day; you just have to be willing to see them.

How many marks are in your notebook? _____

(share with your spouse).

CHALLENGE DAY NINE COMPLETE

Challenge Day Ten Declaration

We speak in agreement that God will rule and maintain authority over our marriage. We touch and agree that there will be no other voice other than God that will have leverage in our relationship. We declare today that God loves us and personally keeps our relationship strong by the power of His Word and the Love that can only come from a loving God. We will keep our minds on the Lord and declare victory over any situation that threatens our relationship!

Today, we will not complain.

Where Do You Want To Be In 10 yrs, 20 yrs, 30 yrs, etc.?

... Oh, that all the Lord's people were prophets and that the Lord would put His Spirit upon them! Numbers 11:29

DISCUSSION TOPIC
(Pray before each discussion that God will bring back the best memories)

Do you have a plan for your family? Have you and your spouse had a discussion about exactly where you want to see your family in the future? Do you want to live in the suburbs, the city, the country… maybe on a farm? Have you talked about retirement? Do you want more children? (it's ok to laugh if you don't) Do you want to live in a big house (a smaller house)? Do you want to travel? If so, where would you like to go first? How do you picture your old age with your spouse?

Do you feel like an eagle in a chicken coop? Do you feel like the lion in the kitty box? You know in your mind and heart that there is so much more within than what you are experiencing and expressing in your life right now. You feel certain that God has a greater purpose for *your* life and for your marriage (and you can't seem to escape the urge to "go for it"). We are encouraging you today to take the leap. Spread your wings. Never give up on the greatness that you and your spouse were created to do and to achieve together. Realize your passion and hunger for achievement are from God and placed within you and your spouse together. Recognize, right now… at this very moment that together, you can achieve ANYTHING! Yes, You ARE a lion! Feel free to roar!

DAILY PRAYER

Before you start your day, before you leave your room in the morning hold hands and PRAY (read together and then add your own words of love and support for your spouse):

Father, thank You for my spouse and for the unique and amazing gifts and abilities you've placed in our relationship. Help us to appreciate them and focus on the strengths more than the weaknesses. Allow us to see the best in our spouse and to notice and remember all of the wonderful reasons we chose to connect and marry. Today, we choose to be a blessing and let You take care of everything else, including our future. We trust you, Lord. AMEN.

MARRIAGE CHALLENGE

We challenge you to start a marriage journal together. Write down all of the things you want to remember about your relationship (only write positive things in the journal). Take time to dream about the future. Share your thoughts with one another.

Remember to follow this recipe to the letter. It's not about the meal; it's about the *priority time* that you spend together.

No complaining, not whining, just enjoy your time with one another.

Pastor Chefs Sweet Potato Mac & Cheese

Ingredients

8 ounces whole-wheat elbow noodles (2 cups)
1 medium sweet potato (about 12 ounces)
2 cups nonfat milk
2 tablespoons all-purpose flour
1 small clove garlic, minced
1 Serenade
1 1/4 cups shredded sharp Cheddar cheese
1 tablespoon Dijon mustard
1/4 teaspoon salt
1/4 teaspoon freshly ground pepper
1/2 cup frozen peas, thawed
3 tablespoons coarse dry whole-wheat breadcrumbs (see Tip)
1 teaspoon extra-virgin olive oil

Preparation

Position a rack in upper third of oven; preheat broiler. Coat a 2-quart broiler-safe baking dish with cooking spray.

Cook noodles in a large pot of boiling water until just tender, 7 to 9 minutes. Drain; set aside.

Meanwhile, prick sweet potato with a fork in several places. Microwave on High until tender all the way to the center, 7 to 10 minutes.

Whisk milk, flour and garlic in a large saucepan. Heat over medium heat, whisking frequently, until steaming and hot, but not boiling. Remove from heat.

As soon as the sweet potato is cool enough to handle, cut open and scoop the flesh into the steaming milk. Puree with an immersion blender until smooth. (Alternatively, transfer to a blender and puree just until smooth, then return to the pot; use caution when pureeing hot liquids.) Add cheese, mustard, salt and pepper and stir until the cheese melts. Add the pasta and peas to the sauce and stir to coat. Transfer to the prepared baking dish. Combine breadcrumbs and oil and sprinkle on the pasta. Broil on the upper rack until the top is lightly browned and crispy, 1 to 2 minutes

While sitting down to dinner, husband serenade your wife…. Ok wife, dance to the song your husband is singing (remember, have fun… no complaining!)

Day Ten Challenge Reflection

The Pastor Chef NO COMPLAINING Challenge is 21 days of PRAYING together, DISCUSSING daily topics, READING together, COOKING together and Holding one another ACCOUNTABLE to the concept of not complaining. Then close the day with a FAMILY DECLARATION!!!

It's not enough for couples to just stop complain, couples need to master counting their blessings **as a couple** from day to day.

HOW TO COUNT YOUR DAILY BLESSINGS

Below are three simple ways to count your blessings as a couple every day:

1) **Journal your blessings all through the day.** Rather than saving your gratitude journal activities for bedtime only, why not make them an ongoing activity all day long? **Keep a small notebook and pencil in your pocket and <u>write a quick note every time something positive happens</u>.**

Little things matter! The more you focus on them, the more you'll begin to feel grateful about the bigger things too. Be prepared to share every positive experience with your spouse.

Quick List for your daily Discussion: (you may need more paper) _____

_____

_____

_____

_____

_____

_____

2) Just like you can journal your positive experiences, you can make it your mission to find something positive about difficult situations. <u>Using the same little notebook</u>, **every time you encounter a challenge or seemingly negative situation, find at least one positive thing you can say about it and write it down**. (at least try)

Quick List for your daily Discussion: _____

_____

_____

_____

_____

3) Finally, you could **literally count your blessings**. Rather than recording the specifics, **simply make a mark in your notebook** every time you experience something to feel grateful about. At the end of the day, glance over your page of marks. How many are there? Make a note of the number and then try to beat it each day afterwards. There are literally thousands of possible things to be grateful about in the course of a single day; you just have to be willing to see them.

How many marks are in your notebook? _____
(share with your spouse).

CHALLENGE DAY TEN COMPLETE

CHALLENGE DAY 11

Challenge Day Eleven Declaration

We declare that our marriage and relationship is complete and satisfying. We declare that God is taking our marriage to a new level of maturity. We have made up our minds that we will enjoy every moment of our time together. We will not accept failure or defeat in our relationship. We have confidence that God is taking us to new levels of joy and peace in our marriage. TODAY, I am completely satisfied in my marriage and my relationship.

Today, we will not complain.

Do you remember how you chose your children's names? (If you don't have children... what do you want to name them? Why?)

As a father has compassion on his children, so the LORD has compassion on those who fear him. Psalms 103:13

DISCUSSION TOPIC
(Pray before each discussion that God will bring back the best memories)

Do you remember the conversation you had to name your children? Do you remember the other name options? Do you remember the best (the funniest) name? What do your children's names mean? If you don't have children, what would you want to name them? (boy name, girl name) What do you think your name means? Do you think your name fits you? If you could choose another name, what would you choose? What would be good names for twins?

God does not expect for any of us to be perfect. In fact, it is precisely the very reason he sent Jesus and the Holy Spirit to help us in our daily lives. If we could do it all by ourselves, we would not need God's help and support at all. Thankfully, Jesus came to forgive us our imperfections and to wipe away all of our sins and weaknesses from God's sight. Through Jesus Christ we are actually perfect, and through His name our marriages and relationships can be perfect too. We can never achieve that real level of love and peace through our own strength and performance. God does not expect our relationships with one another to always be perfect, but He does expect for us to grow together in Him, perfectly. Trusting God and maturing in His name will take any marriage a long way.

DAILY PRAYER

Before you start your day, before you leave your room in the morning hold hands and PRAY (read together and then add your own words of love and support for your spouse):

Father, We are so thankful that you are taking our relationship and helping us to grow into a spiritually complete and mature relationship. We are not perfect, but because of Your work and sacrifice for our relationship and life, we thank You that we are okay and we are on our way to living in and enjoying a much much more mature and healthy relationship. AMEN.

MARRIAGE CHALLENGE

If you have children tell them why you gave them the names you gave them. Share with them the story and enjoy the moment with your family. If you don't have children invite friends over, tell them the story (share your future names). Have fun... No complaining.

Remember to follow this recipe to the letter. It's not about the meal; it's about the *priority time* that you spend together.

No complaining, not whining, just enjoy your time with one another.

Pastor Chefs Quinoa Pilaf with Seared Scallops

Ingredients

2 tablespoons extra-virgin olive oil, divided
3 scallions, sliced, greens and whites separated
1 cup quinoa
1 cup water
2 medium blood oranges or navel oranges
1 long passionate kiss
1/4 cup toasted sliced almonds (see Tip), divided
1/4 cup chopped fresh cilantro
1 teaspoon ground cumin, divided
1/2 teaspoon ground coriander, divided
1/4 teaspoon salt
1 pound dry sea scallops

Preparation

Heat 1 tablespoon oil in a large saucepan over medium-high heat. Add scallion whites; cook, stirring, until beginning to brown, about 1 minute. Add quinoa; cook, stirring until toasted and fragrant, about 1 minute more. Add water; bring to a boil. Reduce heat, cover and simmer until tender, 10 to 15 minutes. Let stand, covered, for 5 minutes.

Meanwhile, slice ends off oranges. With a sharp knife, remove the peel and white pith; discard. Working over a large bowl, cut the orange segments from their surrounding membranes. Squeeze juice from the membranes into the bowl before discarding them, if desired. Add the scallion greens, almonds, cilantro, 1/2 teaspoon cumin, 1/4 teaspoon coriander and salt to the bowl; gently stir to combine.

Pat scallops dry and sprinkle both sides with the remaining 1/2 teaspoon cumin and 1/4 teaspoon coriander. Add 1 long passionate kiss. Heat the remaining 1 tablespoon oil in a large cast-iron or nonstick skillet over medium-high heat. Add the scallops and cook until golden brown, 2 to 3 minutes per side. (To prevent overcooking, transfer the scallops to a plate as soon as they are done.)

Add the quinoa to the bowl with the orange mixture and gently stir to combine. Serve the scallops over the warm quinoa salad.

When was the last time you just laughed together, without other people being around? We challenge you to make your spouse laugh out loud! (it's ok to be silly)

Day Eleven Challenge Reflection

The Pastor Chef NO COMPLAINING Challenge is 21 days of PRAYING together, DISCUSSING daily topics, READING together, COOKING together and Holding one another ACCOUNTABLE to the concept of not complaining. Then close the day with a FAMILY DECLARATION!!!

It's not enough for couples to just stop complain, couples need to master counting their blessings **as a couple** from day to day.

HOW TO COUNT YOUR DAILY BLESSINGS

Below are three simple ways to count your blessings as a couple every day:

1) **Journal your blessings all through the day.** Rather than saving your gratitude journal activities for bedtime only, why not make them an ongoing activity all day long? **Keep a small notebook and pencil in your pocket and <u>write a quick note every time something positive happens</u>.**

Little things matter! The more you focus on them, the more you'll begin to feel grateful about the bigger things too. Be prepared to share every positive experience with your spouse.

Quick List for your daily Discussion: (you may need more paper) _____

_____

_____

_____

_____

_____

_____

2) Just like you can journal your positive experiences, you can make it your mission to find something positive about difficult situations. <u>Using the same little notebook</u>, **every time you encounter a challenge or seemingly negative situation, find at least one positive thing you can say about it and write it down**. (at least try)

Quick List for your daily Discussion: _____

_____

_____

_____

_____

3) Finally, you could **literally count your blessings**. Rather than recording the specifics, **simply make a mark in your notebook** every time you experience something to feel grateful about. At the end of the day, glance over your page of marks. How many are there? Make a note of the number and then try to beat it each day afterwards. There are literally thousands of possible things to be grateful about in the course of a single day; you just have to be willing to see them.

How many marks are in your notebook? _____

(share with your spouse).

CHALLENGE DAY ELEVEN COMPLETE

CHALLENGE DAY 12

Challenge Day Twelve Declaration

We declare and decree that our family will be blessed and known for having a passion and commitment to serving God. We will not allow our hands to become idle and slack. TODAY we speak prosperity and purpose over our marriage and over our family. We declare that every storm that rises up against us will be stilled and every enemy that speaks against our relationship will be silenced. TODAY, we take the first steps into victorious living!

Today, we will not complain.

Do you remember the first time your spouse cooked a special meal for you?

However, this kind does not go out except by prayer and fasting.
Matthew 17:12

DISCUSSION TOPIC
(Pray before each discussion that God will bring back the best memories)

What did you order on your first dinner date? What was the first thing your spouse cooked for you? What was the first thing you cooked together? What is your favorite dish that your spouse makes? What is your favorite restaurant? (why?) what is your favorite food memory? Do you remember the first time you went to a movie together? (what was the movie?) Do you think that you have a cooking specialty? Do you think your spouse has a cooking specialty? What is your favorite cooking (food) memory?

The entire pastor Chefs concept is laid out on the premise that a couple who READS together, PRAYS together and COOKS together will have stronger marriages. We're not over driven by the cooking part, but we do believe in giving your spouse priority time every single day. That is giving your spouse on a daily basis COMPLETE undivided attention. We live in a busy and hectic society, it's easy to lose sight of just how fragile a marriage can be and just how important it is to tend the relationship each and every day. When your connection is strong with your spouse you honestly feel like there is NOTHING you cannot do, when your connection is weak, everything feels like a strain. Make up your mind, that regardless of your circumstances, you will never stop tending to your relationship and never take it for granted.

DAILY PRAYER

Before you start your day, before you leave your room in the morning hold hands and PRAY (read together and then add your own words of love and support for your spouse):

I thank You, Lord, that You have given us so many daily blessings. Help us Lord to be content and not to take any of them for granted. Help us to focus and tend to our relationship every single day by giving one another personal and priority time together. Even as we wait on You for the various things we are praying for, we choose to be grateful for the blessings that we have in one another each and every day. Thank You, Lord for my spouse. AMEN.

MARRIAGE CHALLENGE

If you remember the first meal that you cooked for your spouse. Cook it again. (Do you think you'll like it just as much? If you remember the first meal that your spouse cooked for you, Cook that one again. (Does it taste any better? are you a better cook now?) Have fun with this one. It's ok to laugh! ... No Complaining.

Remember to follow this recipe to the letter. It's not about the meal; it's about the *priority time* that you spend together.

No complaining, not whining, just enjoy your time with one another.

Pastor Chefs Clementine & Five-Spice Chicken

Ingredients

8-10 Clementine, divided
Generous 1/4 teaspoon Chinese five-spice powder (see Tips)
1/4 teaspoon Szechuan peppercorns, crushed (see Tips, optional)
2 teaspoons canola oil, divided
4 large bone-in chicken thighs (about 2 pounds), skin removed, trimmed
1 teaspoon kosher salt
1 beautiful memory
1/4 cup small fresh cilantro leaves
1 tablespoon thinly sliced scallion greens
1/4 teaspoon toasted sesame oil

Preparation

Finely grate 1 teaspoon zest (see Tips) and squeeze 1 cup juice from 6 to 8 Clementine. Combine the zest, juice, five-spice powder and peppercorns (if using) in a small bowl.

Heat oil in a large nonstick skillet over medium-high heat. Season chicken with salt. Cook the chicken, turning frequently, until brown on both sides, about 5 minutes. Pour in the juice mixture; bring to a simmer. Reduce the heat to maintain a simmer, cover and cook until the chicken is just cooked through, 16 to 18 minutes.

Meanwhile, peel 2 of the remaining Clementine and slice into 1/4-inch-thick rounds.

When the chicken is done, transfer to a plate and tent with foil to keep warm. Increase the heat to high and cook the sauce, stirring often, until thickened and reduced to 1/2 to 2/3 cup, 2 to 4 minutes. Stir in the Clementine slices, cilantro, scallion greens and sesame oil. Serve the chicken with the sauce.

Before eating dinner, share 1 beautiful memory together. Don't forget to set the mood, candles, soft music, maybe where a tux and an evening gown for tonight's meal. (Have fun... Don't complain)

Day Twelve Challenge Reflection

The Pastor Chef NO COMPLAINING Challenge is 21 days of PRAYING together, DISCUSSING daily topics, READING together, COOKING together and Holding one another ACCOUNTABLE to the concept of not complaining. Then close the day with a FAMILY DECLARATION!!!

It's not enough for couples to just stop complain, couples need to master counting their blessings **as a couple** from day to day.

HOW TO COUNT YOUR DAILY BLESSINGS

Below are three simple ways to count your blessings as a couple every day:

1) **Journal your blessings all through the day.** Rather than saving your gratitude journal activities for bedtime only, why not make them an ongoing activity all day long? **Keep a small notebook and pencil in your pocket and <u>write a quick note every time something positive happens</u>.**

Little things matter! The more you focus on them, the more you'll begin to feel grateful about the bigger things too. Be prepared to share every positive experience with your spouse.

Quick List for your daily Discussion: (you may need more paper) _____

_____

_____

_____

_____

_____

_____

_____

2) Just like you can journal your positive experiences, you can make it your mission to find something positive about difficult situations. Using the same little notebook, **every time you encounter a challenge or seemingly negative situation, find at least one positive thing you can say about it and write it down**. (at least try)

Quick List for your daily Discussion: _____

_____

_____

_____

_____

3) Finally, you could **literally count your blessings**. Rather than recording the specifics, **simply make a mark in your notebook** every time you experience something to feel grateful about. At the end of the day, glance over your page of marks. How many are there? Make a note of the number and then try to beat it each day afterwards. There are literally thousands of possible things to be grateful about in the course of a single day; you just have to be willing to see them.

How many marks are in your notebook? _____
(share with your spouse).

CHALLENGE DAY TWELVE COMPLETE

Challenge Day Thirteen Declaration

We declare to the world and shout from the rooftops that the state of our marriage is strong! No weapon formed against us can prosper! No enemy can break through our mighty defenses. Our Marriage can withstand any issue, any obstacle any enemy because we have a God that fights our battles. TODAY, we stand in agreement that we will never back down from our destiny! We will never give up on one another and we will never let our issues become our marriage. We are better than that.

Today, we will not complain.

CHALLENGE DAY 13

Share Your favorite elementary, middle, high school, College memory

However, this kind does not go out except by prayer and fasting.

Matthew 17:12

DISCUSSION TOPIC
(Pray before each discussion that God will bring back the best memories)

Can you remember your first grade teacher? Do you remember your first day of middle school? What about high school? Were you an athlete? Were you a good student? Do you remember your best friends from each grade level? (are you still friend with them now?) Were you a rebellious rule breaker or an unapologetic rule keeper? What was the craziest thing you did in high school/college? Do you remember your first crush? (how has your taste changed over the years?) what was your favorite class? why?

How many millions of people feel as though they were missing out on life in one way or another because they are married and never discussed the future. Unfortunately, you can't actually plan for something you don't talk about. This is when you remember that wishing does not do any good, only action and active discussion changes things. If you are not getting anything out of your marriage, perhaps you are not putting enough into it. If you want your marriage or any other relationship to improve, just start being grateful for that person and try to bless them every chance you get. Leave the past in the past and make up your mind that you're going to spend more time rejoicing over your future than reminiscing about your past glories.

DAILY PRAYER

Before you start your day, before you leave your room in the morning hold hands and PRAY (read together and then add your own words of love and support for your spouse):

We thank You TODAY, Lord, that You are guiding us in this relationship one step at a time. We completely trust Your direction and wisdom for this marriage. We thank you that Your plans for this relationship and connection is good and that you will never lead us astray. We place ALL of our trust and confidence in You, Lord. Amen!

MARRIAGE CHALLENGE

Find your high school yearbook, find yourselves and tell your favorite stories from High School. If you can't find your yearbook, find your camera and dress like you would have in high school. Take picture and create your own yearbook. (oh come on now, you know you want to) Have fun... take lots of picture. No Complaining.

Remember to follow this recipe to the letter. It's not about the meal; it's about the *priority time* that you spend together.

No complaining, not whining, just enjoy your time with one another.

Pastor Chefs Salmon with Toasted Pearl Couscous

Ingredients

1 tablespoon extra-virgin olive oil
1 cup Israeli couscous (see Tip)
1/2 cup finely chopped red bell pepper
1/3 cup unsalted pistachios, coarsely chopped
1 large shallot, chopped
1/2 teaspoon salt, divided
1 1/2 cups water
1 prayer of agreement
1 tablespoon chopped fresh parsley, plus more for garnish
1 tablespoon chopped fresh oregano, plus more for garnish
1 1/4 pounds wild Alaskan salmon fillet, skinned and cut into 4 portions
1/4 teaspoon freshly ground pepper
4 lemon wedges

Preparation

Heat oil in a large nonstick skillet over medium heat. Add couscous, bell pepper, pistachios, shallot and 1/4 teaspoon salt. Cook, stirring frequently, until the couscous is lightly toasted, about 5 minutes. Stir in water. Cover and cook, stirring occasionally, for 5 minutes. Stir in 1 tablespoon each parsley and oregano.

Sprinkle salmon with pepper and the remaining 1/4 teaspoon salt, and 1 prayer of agreement. Place the salmon on top of the couscous, reduce the heat to medium-low, cover and cook until the salmon is cooked through and the water is absorbed, 5 to 7 minutes.

Serve garnished with herbs, if desired, and lemon wedges.

Before you eat, Pray for one another. Share something you've been praying for in your marriage for a long time. Come to agreement… Pray about it. Trust God with the results.

Day Thirteen Challenge Reflection

The Pastor Chef NO COMPLAINING Challenge is 21 days of PRAYING together, DISCUSSING daily topics, READING together, COOKING together and Holding one another ACCOUNTABLE to the concept of not complaining. Then close the day with a FAMILY DECLARATION!!!

It's not enough for couples to just stop complain, couples need to master counting their blessings **as a couple** from day to day.

HOW TO COUNT YOUR DAILY BLESSINGS

Below are three simple ways to count your blessings as a couple every day:

1) **Journal your blessings all through the day.** Rather than saving your gratitude journal activities for bedtime only, why not make them an ongoing activity all day long? **Keep a small notebook and pencil in your pocket and <u>write a quick note every time something positive happens</u>.**

Little things matter! The more you focus on them, the more you'll begin to feel grateful about the bigger things too. Be prepared to share every positive experience with your spouse.

Quick List for your daily Discussion: (you may need more paper) _____

_____

_____

_____

_____

_____

_____

2) Just like you can journal your positive experiences, you can make it your mission to find something positive about difficult situations. Using the same little notebook, **every time you encounter a challenge or seemingly negative situation, find at least one positive thing you can say about it and write it down**. (at least try)

Quick List for your daily Discussion: _____

_____

_____

_____

_____

3) Finally, you could **literally count your blessings**. Rather than recording the specifics, **simply make a mark in your notebook** every time you experience something to feel grateful about. At the end of the day, glance over your page of marks. How many are there? Make a note of the number and then try to beat it each day afterwards. There are literally thousands of possible things to be grateful about in the course of a single day; you just have to be willing to see them.

How many marks are in your notebook? _____

(share with your spouse).

CHALLENGE DAY THIRTEEN COMPLETE

Challenge Day Fourteen Declaration

We declare and speak into our marriage a spirit of freshness and passion. We touch and agree that we will work harder to keep the connection fresh. We have made up our minds that we WILL love and care for one another in our 30th year with the same love and fervor we did on our first day. We declare and decree that the world will be able to see our love for God through our love for one another. Our love for one another will become a direct reflection of our love for the Lord.

Today, we will not complain.

CHALLENGE DAY 14

Remember Your Honeymoon (if you didn't have one, let's pretend)

And we all, who with unveiled faces contemplate the Lord's glory, are being transformed into his image with ever-increasing glory, which comes from the Lord, who is the Spirit. 1 Corinthians 3:18

DISCUSSION TOPIC
(Pray before each discussion that God will bring back the best memories)

Where did you go on your honeymoon? Do you remember the name of the hotel if you stayed at one? What would be your fantasy honeymoon? Share with your spouse your favorite part of your honeymoon? (the part you could share with the children) Was it what you were hoping for? Was it how you imagined it to be? Did your wife where lingerie? (Do you remember what color they were? Describe them.) Did your husband wear a special cologne? Does he still wear it? Do you plan to go on a second, third, fourth honeymoon? What is the most exotic place that you would like to go with your spouse? (do you both agree? Well, then start planning now!)

In marriage, transformation does not happen overnight, and the process can seem very slow at times. But that doesn't change the fact that one of the benefits of living in a relationship with Jesus is the freedom to forget the past and move ahead with your future. The best part of marriage is that it's meant to last a lifetime, through the hardship and through the challenges. Marriage can outlast even the worst situations if you trust God and remember... the honeymoon is just the first day, then the life begins. When you trust God with your relationship, the time it takes to overcome issues is irrelevant. Marriage is a representative of eternity. It starts off young and magical, but its designed to last through every issue and every trial. Sometimes you have to remind yourself, you may not be there yet, but you've taken the first step and you're not going to stop fighting for your legacy till death do us part.

DAILY PRAYER

Before you start your day, before you leave your room in the morning hold hands and PRAY (read together and then add your own words of love and support for your spouse):

Thank you, Father, that You are transforming our lives and our marriage in your perfect timing. We trust You, and we choose not to feel condemned or frustrated any longer. We accept that every day in marriage can't be the honeymoon, but we know that joy is a natural part of eternity and submit our lives and marriage to Your Will. You are at work in our lives and we are grateful for that. Thank You. AMEN.

MARRIAGE CHALLENGE

We challenge you to completely re-live your honeymoon night. (and then go back and re-live your honeymoon day.) try to wear the same things, have the same conversation...Just have fun with this... No complaining.

Remember to follow this recipe to the letter. It's not about the meal; it's about the *priority time* that you spend together.

No complaining, not whining, just enjoy your time with one another.

Pastor Chefs Garlic Shrimp with Cilantro Spaghetti Squash

Ingredients

1 2 1/2- to 3-pound spaghetti squash, halved lengthwise and seeded
2 tablespoons extra-virgin olive oil
1 tablespoon minced garlic
1 teaspoon ground coriander
1 teaspoon ground cumin
1/2 teaspoon salt, divided
1/4 teaspoon cayenne pepper
1 compliment
1/3 cup dry white wine, such as pinot grigio
1 pound peeled and deveined raw shrimp (16-20 per pound), tails left on if desired
1 tablespoon lemon juice
1/4 cup chopped fresh cilantro
2 tablespoons unsalted butter, melted
1/4 teaspoon ground pepper
Lemon wedges for serving

Preparation

Place squash cut-side down in a microwave-safe dish; add 2 tablespoons water. Microwave, uncovered, on High until the flesh is tender, about 10 minutes. (Alternatively, place squash halves cut-side down on a rimmed baking sheet. Bake in a 400°F oven until the squash is tender, 40 to 50 minutes.)

Meanwhile, heat oil in a large skillet over medium-high heat. Add garlic, coriander, cumin, 1/4 teaspoon salt and cayenne; cook, stirring, for 30 seconds. Add wine and bring to a simmer. Add shrimp and cook, stirring, until the shrimp are pink and just cooked through, 3 to 4 minutes. Remove from heat and stir in lemon juice. Add 1 compliment.

Use a fork to scrape the squash from the shells into a medium bowl. Add cilantro, butter, pepper and the remaining 1/4 teaspoon salt; stir to combine. Serve the shrimp over the spaghetti squash with a lemon wedge on the side.

Make dinner simple tonight, go put on your sexiest pajamas and lingerie… sit down, enjoy your meal. (seriously… enjoy the meal).

Day Fourteen Challenge Reflection

The Pastor Chef NO COMPLAINING Challenge is 21 days of PRAYING together, DISCUSSING daily topics, READING together, COOKING together and Holding one another ACCOUNTABLE to the concept of not complaining. Then close the day with a FAMILY DECLARATION!!!

It's not enough for couples to just stop complain, couples need to master counting their blessings **as a couple** from day to day.

HOW TO COUNT YOUR DAILY BLESSINGS

Below are three simple ways to count your blessings as a couple every day:

1) **Journal your blessings all through the day.** Rather than saving your gratitude journal activities for bedtime only, why not make them an ongoing activity all day long? **Keep a small notebook and pencil in your pocket and <u>write a quick note every time something positive happens</u>**.

Little things matter! The more you focus on them, the more you'll begin to feel grateful about the bigger things too. Be prepared to share every positive experience with your spouse.

Quick List for your daily Discussion: (you may need more paper) _____

_____

_____

_____

_____

_____

_____

_____

2) Just like you can journal your positive experiences, you can make it your mission to find something positive about difficult situations. <u>Using the same little notebook,</u> **every time you encounter a challenge or seemingly negative situation, find at least one positive thing you can say about it and write it down**. (at least try)

Quick List for your daily Discussion: _____

_____

_____

_____

_____

3) Finally, you could **literally count your blessings**. Rather than recording the specifics, **simply make a mark in your notebook** every time you experience something to feel grateful about. At the end of the day, glance over your page of marks. How many are there? Make a note of the number and then try to beat it each day afterwards. There are literally thousands of possible things to be grateful about in the course of a single day; you just have to be willing to see them.

How many marks are in your notebook? _____
                                        (share with your spouse).

CHALLENGE DAY FOURTEEN COMPLETE

Challenge Day Fifteen Declaration

We declare and decree joy and laughter into our marriage and relationship. We declare that TODAY we will laugh together, play together and simply enjoy life together. We declare that no storm will rob us from the opportunity to enjoy one another's company and the abundance that can only come from the relationship that God has formed in us. We recognize today that only through Christ can we find real joy in our relationship. We have decided that ALL of our joy and confidence will come from our Lord!

Today, we will not complain.

CHALLENGE DAY 15

If You Won The Lottery, What Would You Do With All That Money?

He who did not spare his own Son, but gave him up for us all— how will he not also, along with him, graciously give us all things? Romans 8:32

DISCUSSION TOPIC
(Pray before each discussion that God will bring back the best memories)

What would you do if you had unlimited funds? Would you travel? Would you buy a bigger house? Would you change the community you live in? Would you give a lot to charity? How would you protect yourself from losing it all? Would unlimited funds help or hurt your marriage? Would you do more together or less together? Would you want to live a more private life or a more public life? Would you want your children to go to a special school? Would you adopt a less fortunate child? Would you go back to school?

Some people seem to have the idea that to be a Christian they have to stop dreaming and fantasizing about more. God is love, He is good, and He wants us to enjoy good things. The Bible says God gives us all things ceaselessly to enjoy. God loves us so much, that he sent His only begotten son, Jesus, to save us from our sins and to give life, and life more abundant. When we receive Jesus, we receive the kingdom of God within us, and the kingdom, is righteousness, peace and joy in the Holy Spirit. We can choose to continue to live with misery, depression, discouragement, fear, worry, anxiety, guilt and condemnation, but Jesus wants us to receive the freedom from those things in exchange for the peace that can only come from His love. Through Jesus, we can actually live an abundant life without unlimited financial wealth.

DAILY PRAYER

Before you start your day, before you leave your room in the morning hold hands and PRAY (read together and then add your own words of love and support for your spouse):

Father, help us to realize that You have nothing but good things in store for our lives and for our relationships. Thank You that even when You correct and instruct us, You are showing us a better way to live. We are grateful for Your goodness and the joyful life we can experience in Your name. Thank You for the abundant life that can only come from our love for You. AMEN.

MARRIAGE CHALLENGE

We challenge you to make a wish list together, dream big, laugh about the possibilities. After you've made the list, now talk about the possibilities and what you could do to actually achieve them. (Have fun with this. No complaining).

Remember to follow this recipe to the letter. It's not about the meal; it's about the *priority time* that you spend together.

No complaining, not whining, just enjoy your time with one another.

Pastor Chefs Fish with Coconut-Shallot Sauce

Ingredients

3 large cloves garlic, chopped
3/4 teaspoon kosher salt, divided
1 Hug
2 tablespoons extra-virgin olive oil, divided
2 tablespoons chopped fresh thyme or 2 teaspoons dried
1/4 teaspoon ground pepper, plus more to taste
1 1/4 pounds mahi-mahi, red snapper or grouper, skinned and cut into 4 portions
2 tablespoons finely chopped shallot
1 cup 'lite' coconut milk
3 generous cups of love
1/4 cup unsweetened coconut chips, toasted
Lime wedges for serving

Preparation

Position rack in upper third of oven; preheat broiler to high. Line a baking sheet or broiler pan with foil and coat with cooking spray.

Mash garlic and 1/2 teaspoon salt on a cutting board with a fork to make a thick paste. Combine with 1 tablespoon oil and add a hug, thyme and teaspoon pepper. Place the fish on the prepared pan and spread the paste on top of it.

Heat the remaining 1 tablespoon oil in a medium skillet over medium heat. Add shallot and cook, stirring, for 30 seconds. Add coconut milk, increase heat to medium-high and bring to a simmer. Reduce heat to medium-low and simmer until reduced to 3/4 cup, about 6 minutes. Season with the remaining 1/4 teaspoon salt and pepper to taste.

Meanwhile, broil the fish until just cooked through, 6 to 8 minutes, add 3 generous cups of love. Spoon the sauce on top, sprinkle with coconut and serve with lime.

We challenge you to find a quiet spot in your house after dinner and just hold one another till you fall asleep in each other's arms. Nothing dramatic, just peace, quiet and romantic.

Day Fifteen Challenge Reflection

The Pastor Chef NO COMPLAINING Challenge is 21 days of PRAYING together, DISCUSSING daily topics, READING together, COOKING together and Holding one another ACCOUNTABLE to the concept of not complaining. Then close the day with a FAMILY DECLARATION!!!

It's not enough for couples to just stop complain, couples need to master counting their blessings **as a couple** from day to day.

HOW TO COUNT YOUR DAILY BLESSINGS

Below are three simple ways to count your blessings as a couple every day:

1) **Journal your blessings all through the day.** Rather than saving your gratitude journal activities for bedtime only, why not make them an ongoing activity all day long? **Keep a small notebook and pencil in your pocket and <u>write a quick note every time something positive happens</u>.**

Little things matter! The more you focus on them, the more you'll begin to feel grateful about the bigger things too. Be prepared to share every positive experience with your spouse.

Quick List for your daily Discussion: (you may need more paper) _____

_____

_____

_____

_____

_____

_____

2) Just like you can journal your positive experiences, you can make it your mission to find something positive about difficult situations. <u>Using the same little notebook</u>, **every time you encounter a challenge or seemingly negative situation, find at least one positive thing you can say about it and write it down**. (at least try)

Quick List for your daily Discussion: _____

_____

_____

_____

_____

3) Finally, you could **literally count your blessings**. Rather than recording the specifics, **simply make a mark in your notebook** every time you experience something to feel grateful about. At the end of the day, glance over your page of marks. How many are there? Make a note of the number and then try to beat it each day afterwards. There are literally thousands of possible things to be grateful about in the course of a single day; you just have to be willing to see them.

How many marks are in your notebook? _____

(share with your spouse).

CHALLENGE DAY FIFTEEN COMPLETE

Challenge Day Sixteen Declaration

We declare and decree that love and laughter will always be a part our relationship and our marriage. We declare that a new and refreshing burst of spiritual and emotional joy will fill our home. We speak power, love, peace, joy and laughter into the atmosphere of our home. Joy will become the hallmark of our family. We declare that from this moment forward we will make laughter an active part of our family legacy. We have decided in agreement to laugh much, much more!

Today, we will not complain.

CHALLENGE DAY 16

Do You Have Secret Signals That Only You and Your Spouse Know?

While we do not look at the things which are seen, but at the things which are not seen. For the things which are seen are temporary, but the things which are not seen are eternal. 2 Corinthians 4:18

DISCUSSION TOPIC
(Pray before each discussion that God will bring back the best memories)

Does your spouse have a look that only YOU notice? Do you and your spouse have secret signals that no one else notice? Other than words, how can you tell when your spouse is angry, happy, surprised, disappointed, satisfied (give a complete description to one another)? Do you remember the first time you saw your spouse laugh out loud at a joke? (what did you think?) Share out loud all of the secret signals that you and your wife share. (if you don't have any, take the time to create a few)

Praise God for laughter and for those special moments that only you and your spouse share (what an awesome gift from the Lord!) Laughter and special moments have tremendous power, and this is something everyone would be wise to appreciate and work to laugh that much more. Couples should stop and smell the roses from time to time and learn to appreciate their relationship. If couples just laugh a little bit more (be of good cheer), Couples will find that a bit of laughter makes the various weights they carry just a little bit lighter. In the world we live in it is so easy to find something to worry about, but we can choose to purposely look for things to laugh about sometimes. Take every opportunity you can to laugh and laugh and laugh together!

DAILY PRAYER

Before you start your day, before you leave your room in the morning hold hands and PRAY (read together and then add your own words of love and support for your spouse):

Father, We thank You that Your joy is our strength and that laughter actually works as strong medicine in our relationship. Help us not to carry burdens that You never intended us to carry. Help us to praise the good parts of our relationship and not to stress over any negative. Help us to relax and enjoy the laughter and beauty in our marriage. Thank You, Lord for every joyful moment. AMEN.

MARRIAGE CHALLENGE

We challenge you to play the signals game. See if your spouse can guess the hidden message you're trying to send without words. Try "I'm ready to go" ... "I'm hungry" ... "I'm happy or angry" Enjoy this private time together, make up a few signals of your own, that only YOU would notice. (Have fun with this. No complaining).

Remember to follow this recipe to the letter. It's not about the meal; it's about the *priority time* that you spend together.

No complaining, not whining, just enjoy your time with one another.

Pastor Chefs Charred Lemon Chicken Piccata

Ingredients

2 small lemons, cut into thin rounds
1 1/2 teaspoons sugar (and 1 passionate kiss)
4 garlic cloves, halved
4 (6-ounce) skinless, boneless chicken breast halves, pounded to 3/4-inch thickness
1/2 teaspoon kosher salt, divided
1/2 teaspoon freshly ground black pepper
1 tablespoon olive oil, divided
2 tablespoons unsalted butter, divided
1 teaspoon grated shallot
1/2 teaspoon grated garlic
1 oregano sprig
1 thyme sprig
1/2 cup dry white wine (add an unexpected act of kindness)
1 cup unsalted chicken stock
1 teaspoon all-purpose flour
1 tablespoon capers, rinsed and drained
2 tablespoons chopped fresh flat-leaf parsley

Preparation

Combine lemon slices, sugar, and garlic in a medium bowl. (give your spouse some sugar… a long passionate kiss before you move on)

Sprinkle chicken with 3/8 teaspoon salt and pepper. Heat a large skillet over medium-high heat. Add 2 teaspoons oil; swirl to coat. Add chicken to pan; cook 4 minutes on each side or until done. Place chicken on a plate. Add remaining 1 teaspoon oil to pan; swirl to coat. Add lemon mixture to pan; cook 1 minute or until lemon slices are lightly browned, turning occasionally. Add 1 act of kindness. Return lemon mixture to bowl.

Wipe pan with paper towels. Heat pan over medium heat. Add 1 1/2 teaspoons butter to pan; swirl until butter melts. Add shallot, 1/2 teaspoon grated garlic, oregano sprig, and thyme sprig; cook 1 minute. Add wine to pan, scraping pan to loosen browned bits. Bring to a boil; cook 3 minutes or until liquid almost evaporates. Add remaining 1/8 teaspoon salt, stock, and flour to pan, stirring with a whisk. Bring to a boil; reduce heat, and simmer 3 minutes or until liquid is reduced to about 2/3 cup. Remove pan from heat; discard oregano and thyme sprigs. Stir in remaining 1 1/2 tablespoons butter and capers, stirring until butter melts. Return chicken and any juices to pan; turn to coat with sauce. Top chicken with lemon mixture. Sprinkle with parsley.

We challenge you play a board game with one another (no it doesn't really matter which game you play)… try to win. Have fun with this. No complaining.

Day Sixteen Challenge Reflection

The Pastor Chef NO COMPLAINING Challenge is 21 days of PRAYING together, DISCUSSING daily topics, READING together, COOKING together and Holding one another ACCOUNTABLE to the concept of not complaining. Then close the day with a FAMILY DECLARATION!!!

It's not enough for couples to just stop complain, couples need to master counting their blessings **as a couple** from day to day.

HOW TO COUNT YOUR DAILY BLESSINGS

Below are three simple ways to count your blessings as a couple every day:

1) **Journal your blessings all through the day.** Rather than saving your gratitude journal activities for bedtime only, why not make them an ongoing activity all day long? **Keep a small notebook and pencil in your pocket and <u>write a quick note every time something positive happens</u>.**

Little things matter! The more you focus on them, the more you'll begin to feel grateful about the bigger things too. Be prepared to share every positive experience with your spouse.

Quick List for your daily Discussion: (you may need more paper) _____

_____

_____

_____

_____

_____

_____

2) Just like you can journal your positive experiences, you can make it your mission to find something positive about difficult situations. Using the same little notebook, **every time you encounter a challenge or seemingly negative situation, find at least one positive thing you can say about it and write it down**. (at least try)

Quick List for your daily Discussion: _____

_____

_____

_____

_____

3) Finally, you could **literally count your blessings**. Rather than recording the specifics, **simply make a mark in your notebook** every time you experience something to feel grateful about. At the end of the day, glance over your page of marks. How many are there? Make a note of the number and then try to beat it each day afterwards. There are literally thousands of possible things to be grateful about in the course of a single day; you just have to be willing to see them.

How many marks are in your notebook? _____
                                    (share with your spouse).

CHALLENGE DAY SIXTEEN COMPLETE

CHALLENGE DAY 17

Challenge Day Seventeen Declaration

We Declare and Decree that we will LOVE one another through the good times and the bad. We declare that we will LOVE one another when times are happy or times are sad. We declare that we will LOVE one another without regards to our feelings at the moment. We will stand on God's word and trust Him to strengthen the emotional bond between us. We will use our LOVE as a shield against any and every enemy that comes against our relationship. We will look for reasons to love one another and not for reasons to tear down one another.

Today, we will not complain.

Do You Remember the First Time You Said "I Love You" To Your Spouse?

And so we know and rely on the love God has for us. God is love. Whoever lives in love lives in God, and God in them. 1 John 4:16

DISCUSSION TOPIC
(Pray before each discussion that God will bring back the best memories)

Who said I love you first? Do you remember the first time you heard your spouse tell you that they loved you? What was running through your mind? Do you remember what you were thinking? Was it scary to say? What prompted you to finally say "I love you" to your spouse? Do you remember your spouse's response? (Do they remember it the same way?) When was the last time that you told your spouse that you loved them? Does it have the same meaning for you now as it did the very first time you said it? Do you enjoy hearing it? (saying it?)

The key to trusting God is to know and believe that You are loved by Him. This is also true in a marriage. It's so much easier to trust in your spouse and in your relationship when you believe that your spouse honestly loves you. You cannot expect for your marriage and your relationship to grow when there is no emotional trust, for where there is no emotional trust, there is no safety. The Bible teaches us that nothing can separate us from the love of God in Christ Jesus (see Romans 8:38-39). God wants us to have complete confidence in His love for us. It is also important that you offer your spouse the unconditional love that is grounded in our love for God. Accept God's love for yourself and for your relationship, make that the very foundation for your entire relationship. Then start enjoying yourself in the confidence that the love in your marriage is based on a mature spiritual standard and not an emotional youthful interpretation of feelings.

DAILY PRAYER

Before you start your day, before you leave your room in the morning hold hands and PRAY (read together and then add your own words of love and support for your spouse):

Father, thank You for the gift of Your love! No matter what happens, no matter what we may go through, knowing that You love us and You gave Your only Son for our salvation is all that we need to keep going strong. We are so very grateful for Your Love, and love You, Lord in return. Thank You Lord for allowing us to share this love that can only come from you! AMEN.

MARRIAGE CHALLENGE

We challenge you to tell you spouse that you love them FIFTY (50) times in a single day. Both of you make up your mind that you're going to keep count. (Have fun with this. No complaining).

Remember to follow this recipe to the letter. It's not about the meal; it's about the *priority time* that you spend together.

No complaining, not whining, just enjoy your time with one another.

Pastor Chefs Lemony Chicken Kebabs with Tomato-Parsley Salad

Ingredients

3 tablespoons fresh lemon juice, divided
1 tablespoon minced garlic, divided
1 1/2 teaspoons dried oregano, divided
3/4 teaspoon kosher salt, divided
3/4 teaspoon freshly ground black pepper, divided
3 tablespoons extra-virgin olive oil, divided
4 (6-ounce) skinless, boneless chicken breast halves, cut into 1 1/2-inch cubes
2 cups fresh parsley leaves
Serenade your favorite love song together
1 cup chopped cherry tomatoes

Preparation

Turn facing each other, hold hands, look in each eyes and sing together, your favorite love song.

Combine 2 tablespoons juice, 2 teaspoons garlic, 1 teaspoon oregano, 1/2 teaspoon salt, and 1/2 teaspoon pepper in a bowl. Add 1 tablespoon oil, stirring with a whisk. Add chicken, and stir; marinate in refrigerator 2 hours, covered.

Remove chicken from bowl; discard marinade. Thread chicken onto 4 (10-inch) skewers. Heat a grill pan over high heat. Add skewers; cook 6 minutes or until done, turning often.

Combine remaining 1 tablespoon juice, 1 teaspoon garlic, 1/2 teaspoon oregano, 1/4 teaspoon salt, and 1/4 teaspoon pepper in a medium bowl. Gradually add remaining 2 tablespoons oil, stirring well with a whisk. Add parsley and tomatoes; toss to coat. Serve chicken on top of salad..

We challenge you to pray for and to remember all of the things that you're thankful for in your relationship. Share all the reasons you're convinced that God has been good to you and has been good in your relationship. Write it all down together. Have fun with this one!

Day Seventeen Challenge Reflection

The Pastor Chef NO COMPLAINING Challenge is 21 days of PRAYING together, DISCUSSING daily topics, READING together, COOKING together and Holding one another ACCOUNTABLE to the concept of not complaining. Then close the day with a FAMILY DECLARATION!!!

It's not enough for couples to just stop complain, couples need to master counting their blessings **as a couple** from day to day.

HOW TO COUNT YOUR DAILY BLESSINGS

Below are three simple ways to count your blessings as a couple every day:

1) **Journal your blessings all through the day.** Rather than saving your gratitude journal activities for bedtime only, why not make them an ongoing activity all day long? **Keep a small notebook and pencil in your pocket and <u>write a quick note every time something positive happens</u>.**

Little things matter! The more you focus on them, the more you'll begin to feel grateful about the bigger things too. Be prepared to share every positive experience with your spouse.

Quick List for your daily Discussion: (you may need more paper) _____

_____

_____

_____

_____

_____

_____

_____

2) Just like you can journal your positive experiences, you can make it your mission to find something positive about difficult situations. <u>Using the same little notebook</u>, **every time you encounter a challenge or seemingly negative situation, find at least one positive thing you can say about it and write it down**. (at least try)

Quick List for your daily Discussion: _____

_____

_____

_____

_____

3) Finally, you could **literally count your blessings**. Rather than recording the specifics, **simply make a mark in your notebook** every time you experience something to feel grateful about. At the end of the day, glance over your page of marks. How many are there? Make a note of the number and then try to beat it each day afterwards. There are literally thousands of possible things to be grateful about in the course of a single day; you just have to be willing to see them.

How many marks are in your notebook? _____

(share with your spouse).

CHALLENGE DAY SEVENTEEN COMPLETE

CHALLENGE DAY 18

Challenge Day Eighteen Declaration

We declare and decree that our relationship and connection will change the world! TODAY, we praise God for bringing us together! TODAY, we praise God for the power that can only come from a love like ours! Today we stand in agreement that with God's help we will make a difference in this world! Because God loves us, we will work that much harder to show the world just how much power is in an unwavering love! We stand in the gap for one another and stand in the gap for those who lack the power to pray. We declare TODAY to the entire world that we are in this together!

Today, we will not complain.

Do You Remember the First Time You and Your Spouse Were Intimate?

But earnestly desire the best gifts. And yet I show you a more excellent way. (real love) 1 Corinthians 12:31

DISCUSSION TOPIC
(Pray before each discussion that God will bring back the best memories)

Do you remember the first time you and your spouse were intimate? Where was it? How was it? Share your thoughts on the very first time with your spouse? Has it changed over the years? Do you feel emotionally connected to your spouse? Do you remember the first time you saw your spouse naked? (what did you think?) do you remember the first time you noticed your spouse looking at you while you were naked? (how did it feel?) Do you remember the first conversation you had before/after you were intimate for the very first time?) What makes you feel sexy? What makes you feel loved? What makes you feel close?

Where does love fit into your priorities in your marriage? Where does intimacy fit into your priorities in your marriage? (Do you and your spouse prioritize love and intimacy the same?) Jesus said, "A new commandment I give to you love one another; as I have loved you" (John 13:34) Love and intimacy should have the highest priority in your marital connection. One of the greatest things we have to be thankful for is that God Himself is Love. So when we choose to walk in His love for one another, we are choosing to abide directly in Him. Being intimate with your spouse (physically or emotionally) is a clear expression of your feelings not only for your spouse but also for the God you both serve. Make up your mind that you will not reduce your marital intimacy to mere exercise, allow your time together to be emotional and (yes) spiritual. It is ok for a married couple to pray before sex… and pray after. In fact, … I recommend it.

DAILY PRAYER

Before you start your day, before you leave your room in the morning hold hands

and PRAY (read together and then add your own words of love and support for your spouse):

Father, thank You for the love that You have shown to me. Thank You for the love that my spouse continues to show to me. Thank You for allowing me passionate and emotional intimate moments with my spouse. Thank You for demonstrating that love for me every single day. Help me to receive Your love, and help me to turn around and share that love with my spouse!! Thank You Lord for my continued health and strength. AMEN.

MARRIAGE CHALLENGE

We challenge you to tell you spouse that you love them SIXTY (60) times in a single day. Yes, that is 10 more times than yesterday. Both of you make up your mind that you're going to keep count. (Have fun with this. No complaining).

Remember to follow this recipe to the letter. It's not about the meal; it's about the *priority time* that you spend together.

No complaining, not whining, just enjoy your time with one another.

Pastor Chefs Brazilian Seafood Stew

Ingredients

1 1/2 to 2 lbs of fillets of firm white fish such as halibut, swordfish, cod, or Tilapia rinsed in cold water, pin bones removed, cut into large portions
1 lbs of Shrimp (peeled and deveined) (you can use less/more if you like)
1 lbs of bay scallops (you can use less/more if you like)
3 cloves garlic, minced
4 Tbsp lime or lemon juice
Salt
Freshly ground black pepper
Olive oil
Beautiful memory
1 cup chopped spring onion, or 1 medium yellow onion, chopped or sliced
1/4 cup green onion greens, chopped
1/2 yellow and 1/2 red bell pepper, seeded, de-stemmed, chopped (or sliced) (You can use whole ones if you like)
1 hour cuddle
2 cups chopped (or sliced) tomatoes (Not in a can; Be sure to use fresh firm tomatoes, they are easier to cut)
1 Tbsp paprika (Hungarian sweet) (Regular paprika is fine, Not smoked)
Pinch red pepper flakes
1 large bunch of cilantro, chopped with some set aside for garnish
1 14-ounce can coconut milk (You can use 2 cans if you want to make a larger amount but be sure to double the meat and vegetables if you do)

Preparation

Place fish, shrimp, and scallop pieces in a bowl, add the minced garlic and lime juice so that the pieces are well coated. Sprinkle generously all over with salt and pepper. Keep chilled while preparing the rest of the stew.

In a large covered pan (such as a Dutch oven), coat the bottom with about 2 Tbsp of olive oil and heat on medium heat. Add the chopped onion and cook a few minutes until softened. Add the bell pepper, paprika, and red pepper flakes. Sprinkle generously with salt and pepper. (At least a teaspoon of salt) Cook for a few minutes longer, until the bell pepper begins to soften. Stir in the chopped tomatoes and greens onion (scallions). Bring to a simmer and cook for 5 minutes, uncovered. Stir in the chopped cilantro.

Use a large spoon to remove about half of the vegetables (you'll put them right back in). Spread the remaining vegetables over the bottom of the pan to create a bed for the fish, shrimp, and scallops. Arrange the fish, shrimp, and scallop pieces on top of the vegetables. Sprinkle with salt and pepper. Then add back the previously removed vegetables, covering the fish, shrimp, and scallops. Pour coconut milk over the fish, shrimp, scallops, and vegetables.

Bring stew to a simmer, reduce the heat, cover, and let simmer for 15 minutes. While the stew is simmering, share 1 beautiful memory that you experienced together during your marriage. Taste and adjust seasonings. You may need to add more salt (likely), lime or lemon juice, paprika, pepper, or chili flakes to get the stew to the desired seasoning for your taste. Garnish with cilantro. Serve with rice or with crusty bread.

After dinner, cuddle up together on the sofa for 1 hour and dream about your future plans together.

We have always considered intimacy with your spouse as a form of worship. God wants you to be able to enjoy the connection and closeness that comes from an intimate connection. We challenge you to have a long "conversation" about your love life. Yes, talk about it… what do you like? What don't you like? (we know this was the discussion point… have the conversation again) Have fun with this one! No complaining!

Day Eighteen Challenge Reflection

The Pastor Chef NO COMPLAINING Challenge is 21 days of PRAYING together, DISCUSSING daily topics, READING together, COOKING together and Holding one another ACCOUNTABLE to the concept of not complaining. Then close the day with a FAMILY DECLARATION!!!

It's not enough for couples to just stop complain, couples need to master counting their blessings **as a couple** from day to day.

HOW TO COUNT YOUR DAILY BLESSINGS

Below are three simple ways to count your blessings as a couple every day:

1) **Journal your blessings all through the day.** Rather than saving your gratitude journal activities for bedtime only, why not make them an ongoing activity all day long? **Keep a small notebook and pencil in your pocket and <u>write a quick note every time something positive happens</u>**.

Little things matter! The more you focus on them, the more you'll begin to feel grateful about the bigger things too. Be prepared to share every positive experience with your spouse.

Quick List for your daily Discussion: (you may need more paper) _____

_____

_____

_____

_____

_____

_____

2) Just like you can journal your positive experiences, you can make it your mission to find something positive about difficult situations. Using the same little notebook, **every time you encounter a challenge or seemingly negative situation, find at least one positive thing you can say about it and write it down**. (at least try)

Quick List for your daily Discussion: _____

_____

_____

_____

_____

3) Finally, you could **literally count your blessings**. Rather than recording the specifics, **simply make a mark in your notebook** every time you experience something to feel grateful about. At the end of the day, glance over your page of marks. How many are there? Make a note of the number and then try to beat it each day afterwards. There are literally thousands of possible things to be grateful about in the course of a single day; you just have to be willing to see them.

How many marks are in your notebook? _____
(share with your spouse).

CHALLENGE DAY EIGHTEEN COMPLETE

CHALLENGE DAY 19

Do You Remember the First Time You Slow-Danced Together?

Praise Him with the timbrel and dance; Praise Him with stringed instruments and flutes! Praise Him with loud cymbals; Praise Him with clashing cymbals! Let everything that has breath praise the Lord. Praise the Lord! Psalms 150:4-6

We declare and decree spiritual and emotional abundance over our family! We are winners and not losers, we are the head not the tails, we are the first not the last. In our marriage we are overcomers and declare victory over any and every situation we face together! The enemy cannot come between us because we know that our God is with us! We touch and agree that we will never surrender in the face of a challenge, but in God we will stand ready for victory! God has made us to be a team prepared for anything. TODAY, We accept ANY challenge, TOGETHER!

Today, we will not complain.

DISCUSSION TOPIC
(Pray before each discussion that God will bring back the best memories)

Are you a good dancer? Have you and your spouse ever talked about taking dancing classes together? Do you have a favorite song? If your marriage had a theme song, what would it be? What song always makes you think of your spouse? What song always makes you think of your marriage? Do you remember the first time you saw your spouse dance? Do you remember the first time you looked into your spouse's eyes and didn't say anything at all, but enjoy the moment? What is your spouse's favorite song? What is your spouse's musical preference? If you didn't know your spouse, what type of music would you have guessed they would like? Can your spouse sing?

Constantly focusing on problems will prevent a couple from rejoicing and being glad in their relationship. You might have problems, but if you focus on what's good in your relationship, then you will discover there are some good things in your marriage and life as well. There is no such thing as the perfect situation nor the perfect set of circumstances. That's why it's always best to place your joy in the Lord and not on your circumstances. Every couple should learn to stop and enjoy the little things from time to time. It is so easy to forget that you and your spouse have more in your lives than issues and problems. It's easy to forget to stop from time to time and dance, sing, and laugh together. Thankfully, we can choose to learn not to fret or allow anxiety to rule over your marriage, but in everything to give thanks and praise to God. Then the peace that surpasses all understanding will become an active part of your relationship.

DAILY PRAYER

Before you start your day, before you leave your room in the morning hold hands and PRAY (read together and then add your own words of love and support for your spouse):

Father, thank You for the gift of contentment and joy in my marriage. Regardless of the circumstances around us, we choose to praise You and to realize that You are the true source of joy in our relationship. Thank You for Your goodness and mercy over our marriage and over our lives. We choose to put our hope in You, Lord. We trust You! AMEN.

MARRIAGE CHALLENGE

We challenge you to write a personal song for your spouse and sing it (no you don't have to have the best voice) Serenade your spouse with your new and original love songs. (Have fun with this. No complaining).

Remember to follow this recipe to the letter. It's not about the meal; it's about the *priority time* that you spend together.

No complaining, not whining, just enjoy your time with one another.

Pastor Chefs Tenderloin Steaks with Red Onion Marmalade

Ingredients

Cooking spray
1 large red onion, sliced and separated into rings (about 2 cups)
2 tablespoons red wine vinegar
2 tablespoons honey
1 act of kindness
1/2 teaspoon salt, divided
1 teaspoon dried thyme
1/4 teaspoon freshly ground black pepper
2 passionate kiss
4 (4-ounce) beef tenderloin steaks, trimmed (1 inch thick)

Preparation

Preheat broiler.

Heat a large nonstick skillet over medium-high heat. Coat pan with cooking spray. Add onion to pan. Cover and cook 3 minutes. Give your spouse 1 act of kindness-some sugar (passionate kiss), Add vinegar, honey, and 1/4 teaspoon salt to pan. Reduce heat, and simmer, uncovered, 8 minutes or until slightly thick, stirring occasionally.

Sprinkle remaining 1/4 teaspoon salt, thyme, and pepper evenly over beef. Place beef on a broiler pan coated with cooking spray; broil 4 minutes on each side or until desired degree of doneness. Serve with onion mixture.

After dinner, dim the lights, set the mood and enjoy a slow and intimate dance together… enjoy the music and the feeling of being in one another's arms. Turn the music off, keep dancing with the music in your head. Enjoy the moment. Have fun with this one! No complaining!

Day Nineteen Challenge Reflection

The Pastor Chef NO COMPLAINING Challenge is 21 days of PRAYING together, DISCUSSING daily topics, READING together, COOKING together and Holding one another ACCOUNTABLE to the concept of not complaining. Then close the day with a FAMILY DECLARATION!!!

It's not enough for couples to just stop complain, couples need to master counting their blessings **as a couple** from day to day.

HOW TO COUNT YOUR DAILY BLESSINGS

Below are three simple ways to count your blessings as a couple every day:

1) **Journal your blessings all through the day.** Rather than saving your gratitude journal activities for bedtime only, why not make them an ongoing activity all day long? **Keep a small notebook and pencil in your pocket and <u>write a quick note every time something positive happens</u>**.

Little things matter! The more you focus on them, the more you'll begin to feel grateful about the bigger things too. Be prepared to share every positive experience with your spouse.

Quick List for your daily Discussion: (you may need more paper) _____

_____

_____

_____

_____

_____

_____

2) Just like you can journal your positive experiences, you can make it your mission to find something positive about difficult situations. Using the same little notebook, **every time you encounter a challenge or seemingly negative situation, find at least one positive thing you can say about it and write it down**. (at least try)

Quick List for your daily Discussion: _____

_____

_____

_____

_____

3) Finally, you could **literally count your blessings**. Rather than recording the specifics, **simply make a mark in your notebook** every time you experience something to feel grateful about. At the end of the day, glance over your page of marks. How many are there? Make a note of the number and then try to beat it each day afterwards. There are literally thousands of possible things to be grateful about in the course of a single day; you just have to be willing to see them.

How many marks are in your notebook? _____

(share with your spouse).

CHALLENGE DAY NINETEEN COMPLETE

CHALLENGE DAY 20

Challenge Day Twenty Declaration

We declare and decree that our marriage will be a solid example of love, prayer and constant surrender to a loving and living God. We will never forget the legacy of love, faith and truth that we want our children and the world to see. We commit that our lives and our relationship will be grounded in our faith and strengthened by our integrity and loyalty to our God, our marriage, and to one another. We declare to the World that our marriage is solid and ready for service in the Kingdom of God.

Today, we will not complain.

Do You Remember the First Night in Your Own Home Together?

Your word is a lamp to my feet And a light to my path. Psalms 119:105

DISCUSSION TOPIC
(Pray before each discussion that God will bring back the best memories)

Do you remember your first night together as husband and wife? Do you remember your first night in your own home? Do you remember the address of your first place together? Do you remember the color of the furniture? Do you remember how you found your first home? What was the first meal you cooked in your first new home? What was the first piece of furniture that you purchased? Did you have a pet? (If you didn't what pet would you have had if you could go back and do it again?) What was your first housewarming gift? (Did you like it?) If you could go back and live in your first home again… would you do it? What was the LAST room in your first home that you chose to furnish? (Why was it last?)

Couples with positive minds (minds full of love, faith and hope) produce positive relationships. Couples with negative minds (minds full of fear, confusion and doubt) produce negative relationships. The power of God's words is actually active by faith and clear belief (see Matthew 8:13). Little faith can become great faith if you choose to actually use it. As you take steps in agreement to trust God, Couples experience His faithfulness and that, in turn encourages us to have even greater faith as a couple. As our faith develops and grows, our problems have less power over our relationship and we worry much less. That's something to honestly be thankful for. If we constantly think about the difficulty of our situation we will always find ourselves frustrated in our connections. We may not see the way out or see the next step in life, but just like there was a next step from your first home together, God has a next step for you right now. Trust Him!

DAILY PRAYER

Before you start your day, before you leave your room in the morning hold hands

and PRAY (read together and then add your own words of love and support for your spouse):

Father, I thank You that our faith and connection as a couple can grow stronger and stronger as we put our trust in You! You are greater than any problem we will ever face. When we focus on You, we know that worry and despair will fade away. Thank You for Your faithfulness and Your work in our lives. We trust You and commit to have You, Lord as the foundation of our relationship! AMEN.

MARRIAGE CHALLENGE

We challenge you to go back and visit your old neighborhood. If you can't go back to your original neighborhood, pull out pictures and reminisce. Talk about all the changes you notice. (Have fun with this. No complaining).

Remember to follow this recipe to the letter. It's not about the meal; it's about the *priority time* that you spend together.

No complaining, not whining, just enjoy your time with one another.

Pastor Chefs Roasted Shrimp and Broccoli

Ingredients

5 cups broccoli florets
1 tablespoon grated lemon rind, divided
1 tablespoon fresh lemon juice
1/2 teaspoon salt, divided
1 special ingredient below
1/2 teaspoon freshly ground black pepper, divided
1 1/2 pounds peeled and deveined large shrimp
Cooking spray
2 tablespoons extra-virgin olive oil
1/4 teaspoon crushed red pepper

Preparation

Preheat oven to 425°.

Cook broccoli in boiling water 1 minute. Drain and plunge into ice water; drain.

Combine 1 1/2 teaspoons rind, juice, 1/4 teaspoon salt, and 1/4 teaspoon black pepper in a medium bowl. Add shrimp; toss to combine. Arrange broccoli and shrimp in a single layer on a jelly-roll pan coated with cooking spray. Bake at 425° for 8 minutes or until shrimp are done.

Combine oil, remaining 1 1/2 teaspoons rind, remaining 1/4 teaspoon salt, remaining 1/4 teaspoon black pepper, and crushed red pepper in a large bowl. Add broccoli; toss to combine.

Just like many of you did when you were young, build a makeshift tent in your living room area.... Eat your dinner inside of the tent, enjoy the conversation and the freshness of feeling young again. Have fun! No Complaining!

Day Twenty Challenge Reflection

The Pastor Chef NO COMPLAINING Challenge is 21 days of PRAYING together, DISCUSSING daily topics, READING together, COOKING together and Holding one another ACCOUNTABLE to the concept of not complaining. Then close the day with a FAMILY DECLARATION!!!

It's not enough for couples to just stop complain, couples need to master counting their blessings **as a couple** from day to day.

HOW TO COUNT YOUR DAILY BLESSINGS

Below are three simple ways to count your blessings as a couple every day:

1) **Journal your blessings all through the day.** Rather than saving your gratitude journal activities for bedtime only, why not make them an ongoing activity all day long? **Keep a small notebook and pencil in your pocket and <u>write a quick note every time something positive happens</u>.**

Little things matter! The more you focus on them, the more you'll begin to feel grateful about the bigger things too. Be prepared to share every positive experience with your spouse.

Quick List for your daily Discussion: (you may need more paper) _____

_____

_____

_____

_____

_____

_____

2) Just like you can journal your positive experiences, you can make it your mission to find something positive about difficult situations. Using the same little notebook, **every time you encounter a challenge or seemingly negative situation, find at least one positive thing you can say about it and write it down**. (at least try)

Quick List for your daily Discussion: _____

_____

_____

_____

_____

3) Finally, you could **literally count your blessings**. Rather than recording the specifics, **simply make a mark in your notebook** every time you experience something to feel grateful about. At the end of the day, glance over your page of marks. How many are there? Make a note of the number and then try to beat it each day afterwards. There are literally thousands of possible things to be grateful about in the course of a single day; you just have to be willing to see them.

How many marks are in your notebook? _____

(share with your spouse).

CHALLENGE DAY TWENTY COMPLETE

Challenge Day Twenty One Declaration

We declare and decree that we are grateful for our marriage. We are thankful for the Love that shines in our relationship. We declare love and power in every corner of our marriage and embrace the anointing assigned to our relationship. We speak generational blessing over our household and over our children. We declare that we will appreciate and recognize the positive parts of our marriage and not spend one more moment on the few negative components. We declare that from this moment on we will achieve great things in this life and for the Kingdom of God.

Today, we will not complain.

CHALLENGE DAY 21

Count Your Blessings, Name them One by One!

Whoever guards his mouth and tongue Keeps his soul from troubles..
Proverbs 21:23

DISCUSSION TOPIC
(Pray before each discussion that God will bring back the best memories)

Over the last 21 days you've been asked to keep track and count of the number of times that you felt blessed during the day. Add up all the blessings from all 21 days. Was this number larger than you expected? Now add you and your spouse's number together. After seeing the number, did you realize just how blessed you were? Do you and your spouse pray together on a daily basis? Do you pray together in the morning or the evening? Do you share the number of times you're blessed on a regular day? (or are you working on developing a new habit?) Do you think that you and your spouse are appreciative of the life God has given you? Do you appreciate your spouse?

Transformation doesn't happen overnight, and the process can seem very very slow at times. But that doesn't change the fact that one of the real benefits of trusting God is the freedom to forget and let go of the past and move ahead into what God has prepared just for you. When you find yourself tempted to condemn yourself over the progress that you think you should be making in your relationship, turn your focus back on God's love for you and be thankful that He is doing His work in your life and in your relationship. Trust God's timing for your life and marriage. Remember that with faith ANYTHING is possible, and even though you may not have arrived at the perfection you were expecting, God is not finished with you (nor your relationship) just yet. Trust Him.

DAILY PRAYER

Before you start your day, before you leave your room in the morning hold hands and PRAY (read together and then add your own words of love and support for your spouse):

Thank You, Dear Lord, that You are transforming our relationship in your perfect timing. I trust You, and we choose not to feel condemned or frustrated with one another or the time things are taking any longer. You (oh Lord) are at work in our lives and in our marriage, and we are so grateful for that! We praise You, and we thank You!! AMEN.

MARRIAGE CHALLENGE

You've just finished 21 days of not complaining... We challenge you to go ONE MORE DAY without complaining, create your own discussion topic, pray together, create your own AMAZING recipes together and most importantly COUNT YOUR BLESSINGS!!! (Have fun. Don't forget... No complaining).

Remember to follow this recipe to the letter. It's not about the meal; it's about the *priority time* that you spend together.

No complaining, not whining, just enjoy your time with one another.

Pastor Chefs Black Bean Chili

Ingredients

1 lbs. ground turkey or ground beef
1 small onion, chopped
3 garlic cloves, minced
2 red bell peppers, chopped
1 tablespoon olive oil
3 tablespoons cornmeal
2 tablespoons chili powder
1 hour of cuddling
2 tablespoons smoked paprika
1 tablespoon sugar
1/2 teaspoon ground cumin
2 tablespoon dried oregano
1 tablespoon sea salt
1/4 to 1/2 teaspoon cayenne pepper
2 cans (28 ounces) crushed tomatoes, un-drained
3 can (16 ounces) black beans, rinsed and drained

Preparations

Brown ground turkey or ground beef then set aside. In a Dutch oven on medium heat, saute onion and red bell pepper in oil until tender. Add garlic; cook 1 minute longer. Add the cornmeal. Add ground turkey/beef back into the pot, stir in tomatoes and black beans, add chili powder, sea salt, smoked paprika, sugar, cumin and cayenne; cook and stir.

Bring to a boil. Reduce heat; cover and simmer for 30-45 minutes. Garnish each serving with sour cream, green onions and cilantro.

Add 1 hour of cuddling while eating your chili

Count your blessings, name them one by one. Name them together! Have fun! No Complaining!

Day Twenty One Challenge Reflection

The Pastor Chef NO COMPLAINING Challenge is 21 days of PRAYING together, DISCUSSING daily topics, READING together, COOKING together and Holding one another ACCOUNTABLE to the concept of not complaining. Then close the day with a FAMILY DECLARATION!!!

It's not enough for couples to just stop complain, couples need to master counting their blessings **as a couple** from day to day.

HOW TO COUNT YOUR DAILY BLESSINGS

Below are three simple ways to count your blessings as a couple every day:

1) **Journal your blessings all through the day.** Rather than saving your gratitude journal activities for bedtime only, why not make them an ongoing activity all day long? **Keep a small notebook and pencil in your pocket and <u>write a quick note every time something positive happens</u>.**

Little things matter! The more you focus on them, the more you'll begin to feel grateful about the bigger things too. Be prepared to share every positive experience with your spouse.

Quick List for your daily Discussion: (you may need more paper) _____

_____

_____

_____

_____

_____

_____

2) Just like you can journal your positive experiences, you can make it your mission to find something positive about difficult situations. Using the same little notebook, **every time you encounter a challenge or seemingly negative situation, find at least one positive thing you can say about it and write it down**. (at least try)

Quick List for your daily Discussion: _____

_____

_____

_____

_____

3) Finally, you could **literally count your blessings**. Rather than recording the specifics, **simply make a mark in your notebook** every time you experience something to feel grateful about. At the end of the day, glance over your page of marks. How many are there? Make a note of the number and then try to beat it each day afterwards. There are literally thousands of possible things to be grateful about in the course of a single day; you just have to be willing to see them.

How many marks are in your notebook? _____

(share with your spouse).

CHALLENGE DAY TWENTY ONE COMPLETE

**You have officially completed the 21 days of challenge.
This challenge was designed to press you and your spouse to spend quality
and priority time together.**

A Good Marriage is worth the Challenge

As we said in our previous Pastor Chefs book: "Never forget that marriage is not a fantasy; Marriage is NOT a covenant love affair; it is a covenant "bond" where God forms one person out of two completely different people." Please never forget: SUCCESSFUL MARRIAGES TAKE WORK... SOMETIMES... A LOT OF HARD WORK, BUT IT'S WORTH IT!

There is no magic to success; there is just commitment and clarity that God put you and your spouse together. After 30 plus years of marriage I've come to realize that love combined with a LOT OF stubbornness and priority time can go a long way to helping you get through the hard times.

This is not the end, if you've completed the challenge and want to continue to spend time with your spouse in the kitchen, feel free to look for more pastor chef recipes on Facebook: https://www.facebook.com/PastorChefs

This is how marriages grow stronger... they pray together...they read together... and they COOK together.

We hope you enjoyed **Pastor Chefs 21 Day No Complaining Marriage Challenge** by Bill and Cynthia Malone and that you found it helpful and rewarding in blessing your marriage.

For similar uplifting books from Signalman Publishing, please visit our website at www.signalmanpublishing.com.

Bulk orders are available for discount direct from the publisher. Please contact via email: info@signalmanpublishing.com.

SIGNALMAN
PUBLISHING

www.ingramcontent.com/pod-product-compliance
Lightning Source LLC
LaVergne TN
LVHW081346060426
835508LV00017B/1433